A SAINSBURY CO

THE LOW-FAT *Gourmet*

CAROLINE WALDEGRAVE

CONTENTS

Published exclusively for J Sainsbury plc
Stamford House Stamford Street
London SE1 9LL
by Martin Books
Simon & Schuster Consumer Group
Fitzwilliam House 32 Trumpington Street
Cambridge CB2 1QY

ISBN 0 85941 539 2

First published 1987
Sixth impression October 1991

Printed in Italy by Printer Trento

THE AUTHOR

Caroline Waldegrave trained at the Cordon Bleu School and then went to work for Leith's Good Food, an outside catering company owned by Prue Leith. In 1975, she and Prue Leith set up Leith's School of Food and Wine, where she is currently Managing Director and part-time Principal. Her previous publications include *Leith's Cookery Course* and *Leith's Cookery School,* both in conjunction with Prue Leith, *The Healthy Gourmet* and the Sainsbury Guide *Basic Cooking Skills*. Caroline has long been interested in healthy good food and is a member of the Health Education Authority. She lives in London with her husband, William Waldegrave MP, and their three children.

I would like to thank Sally Procter, Deborah Major, Prue Leith and Maureen Flynn. Most importantly I should like to thank my husband for eating his way through successes and failures alike.

Caroline Waldegrave

INTRODUCTION

I have been interested in healthy eating since I was first pregnant in 1980. I met Christopher Robbins, the then director of the Coronary Prevention Group, and he taught me a great deal about diet and nutrition. I am first and foremost a cook, not a nutritionist, but I set out to learn enough about the science of healthy eating to let me teach students about healthy food, to bring up three children on a healthy diet and to keep my husband in reasonably healthy shape.

You may be perplexed by the apparently dramatic changes of mind which nutritionists have made in the last few years. There have been considerable advances in knowledge which have led to changes in the advice they give, but they are also responding to changing social conditions. Earlier this century, the average national diet was high in inexpensive carbohydrate foods like bread and potatoes and often dangerously low in more costly protein foods like meat. The more affluent post-war years have seen a dramatic change in the way the nation eats, however, and now the danger is seen to be, not exactly too much protein, but too much fat in the diet from high-protein foods like meat and cheese as well as from the obvious sources of fat like butter and cream. Moreover we no longer eat enough carbohydrate to provide adequate dietary fibre.

This is especially true of entertaining and special occasion eating: for most people in this country, these are the cue for special dishes which very often contain a lot of butter, cream and other rich, high-fat ingredients. The aim of this book is to show how the most discriminating cook can give his or her guests the sophisticated food they expect without loading them with fat and calories. By using new skills and techniques, by knowing what is in the food you buy and by combining food in new ways you can produce healthy menus for the choosiest of gourmets, probably without their noticing that you are doing them good.

The changes in diet that I am promoting are not very dramatic, more a shift in emphasis, and the benefits are almost too well known to need justification: fewer calories help to prevent obesity, which is thought to contribute to cardiovascular disease, as does a high fat intake, especially of saturated fat. A low-fat diet is likely to be low also in sugar and salt, which we also need to cut down on, and high in fibre, which aids slimming and helps to protect against gastro-intestinal disorders.

We are told now to reduce our intake of *saturated fat,* but we are also sometimes told that a small increase in *polyunsaturated fat* may be a good thing. What is the difference between these two types of fat? It is a matter of the chemical structure of the *fatty acids* that make them up. Fatty acids are long chains of carbon atoms joined by a chemical bond, which may be either double or single. A fatty acid with no double bonds is called *saturated;* where there is only one double bond it is known as *mono-unsaturated* and where there are two or more, *polyunsaturated.* Most fats are made up of a mixture of many fatty acids. For example, the fat in butter is 63 per cent saturated, three per cent polyunsaturated and 34 per cent mono-unsaturated fatty acids. So when you hear that butter is a 'saturated fat', what it really means is that it is higher in saturated fat than in any other kind. Unsaturated bonds can be converted back into single (saturated) bonds by a process called hydrogenation; a food that undergoes this process, therefore, will become higher in saturated fats. Hydrogenation is used in some food refining processes to make liquid fats solidify.

Why are saturated fats considered now to be 'bad for us'? Medical research suggests that a high level of saturated fat in the blood blocks and damages the arteries and impedes blood circulation. This increases the risk of cardio-vascular disease, which is one of the major killers in this country. Polyunsaturated fat makes the blood less 'sticky' and so prevents it from attaching itself to arterial walls and causing blockages. Thus it has a beneficial effect on health, unless you eat so much of it that your weight starts to become a health problem! Mono-unsaturated fat has no effect on the blood.

Saturated fat is also thought to be a factor in the level of cholesterol in the blood. Cholesterol is commonly a source of confusion. It is a substance associated with fat and can originate in two ways.

Blood (serum) cholesterol is manufactured by the human liver and is an essential part of all healthy cells. The liver makes enough cholesterol for our needs and a high level of saturated fat in the diet makes the liver produce more cholesterol than is needed by the body, in some people.

Dietary cholesterol is cholesterol found in foods. Animal foods which are high in saturated fat are also high in cholesterol and some low-fat foods contain high levels as well. You should be concerned about eating too much fat overall, but not about eating prawns, brains, liver and kidney which, although high in cholesterol, are low in other fats. The important point is still to reduce the proportion of saturated fats in your diet.

All fat is 'fattening', that is, high in calories: a gram of fat releases nine calories, while a gram of carbohydrate releases only four. Calories are a unit of heat energy, but if the food you eat releases more calories than you need your body will store the extra energy as body fat. If you are trying to lose weight, cutting fats out of your diet is therefore the best way. You would find it hard, and it would be foolish, however, to cut them out entirely, as some intake of fat is essential to several metabolic processes.

It is now recommended that no more than 30–35 per cent of daily calories should come from fats of any sort, even if you are not trying to lose weight. Fat in the diet comes from many sources, from the obvious fatty foods such as butter, cream and cheese to 'hidden' sources such as many ready-prepared and processed foods. Meat products, such as sausages, pork pies and so on, are generally high in fat, and especially high in saturates. Some cuts of meat are very fatty and, again, the fat is mostly saturated. The leanest meats are chicken – especially when skinned – turkey, rabbit, game, liver and kidney. Many fish, such as tuna, salmon, herrings and mackerel, are oily, but the fat is mainly mono-unsaturated and poly-unsaturated. If you buy fish canned in oil, however, drain away the oil as it may be high in saturated fat unless, for example, soya oil is used. White fish and shellfish are low in fat.

Low-fat Gourmet Cooking

It isn't possible to do without fat entirely in cooking. In this book I have tried to show how to cook using as little fat as possible; I haven't stuck to a rigid definition of what constitutes low-fat cooking in terms of grams of fat per serving, but tried to give recipes in which the fat content is much lower than it would be in a conventional recipe of the same type.

I avoid the saturated fats in my cooking. This means I do not use butter, lard, cream, dripping, coconut oil, blended cooking fat, mixed blended vegetable oil, solid vegetable fat, or margarines unless they are labelled 'high in polyunsaturated fat'. For general cooking purposes I use sunflower or grapeseed oil as they are both high in polyunsaturated fat. Corn oil is also a good choice but it has a strong flavour, and safflower is high in polyunsaturated fat but very expensive. For special occasions, I buy walnut oil as it is fairly high in polyunsaturated fat and tastes delicious, as does hazelnut oil, which is high in mono-unsaturated fatty acids. I also like to use extra-virgin olive oil, which is high in mono-unsaturated fatty acids. Use a polyunsaturated margarine instead of butter, but don't try using a low-fat spread in cooking, because these tend to separate on contact with heat.

When cooking conventionally, cream is often

an important part of a recipe. Cream is high in saturated fat, so I use low-fat natural yogurt, buttermilk, low-fat soft cheese (quark), tofu, fromage frais and cottage cheese in place of cream. Sainsbury's sell a half-fat cottage cheese.

Sainsbury's also sell a number of products which can be used as substitutes for cream, for example, buttermilk is excellent for enriching soups. Yogurt is very versatile and can be used in breadmaking and soups and it can be served with puddings. Greek yogurt is higher in fat than ordinary natural yogurt but makes a very good cream substitute for special occasions when you would normally serve cream as an accompaniment. Fromage frais and Skimmed Milk Soft Cheese (quark) can both be used for puddings such as cheesecakes as well as dips and pâtés, as can cottage cheese, if it is either sieved or worked in a food processor.

Skimmed milk can easily be substituted for full-fat milk and after a couple of weeks you will not notice the difference. Nuts are a high-fat food although their fat is mainly mono-unsaturated and polyunsaturated. There are two exceptions: coconut is saturated fat and chestnuts are very low in fat.

Of all the foods high in saturated fats, cheese is the one I find hardest to give up. On the whole I try and eat low-fat cheese such as quark or cottage cheese, but for a treat I have Brie and, for a real treat, farmhouse Cheddar. Looking at labels on cheese can be confusing, as in other parts of Europe the fat content is measured at a different stage in the manufacturing process. They measure the amount of fat in the 'dry matter', that is, the fat content of the cheese minus water. Many French cheeses, like Brie, have a high water content. Here in Britain the amount of fat given per 100 g is the amount of fat you actually eat. When you see a Brie labelled in the French way as containing 45 per cent fat it is only about 23 per cent fat by British standards, as a proportion of the whole cheese: that is, the same as the rather bland Edam that dieters have always been told to eat.

Table of fat contents of a few cheeses

Cheese	Fat content (g per 100 g)
Camembert, Brie	23.2
Cheddar, Cheshire, Gruyère, Emmenthal	33.5
Danish Blue, Roquefort	29.2
Edam, Gouda, St Paulin	22.9
Parmesan	29.7
Stilton	40.0
Cream Cheese	47.4

McCance and Widdowson,
The Composition of Foods (Churchill Livingstone, fourth edition)

Sainsbury's sell a 14% cheddar-type hard cheese, a half-fat edam-type and a half-fat grated cheese.

When I changed my diet I realised that I was mostly imitating conventional recipes in a healthier way, making my shepherd's pie with more vegetables and less mince, for example. There are some dishes which you cannot imitate. What is the point of a yogurt-based *crème brulée?* Or a carob, polyunsaturated oil, wholemeal flour and raw sugar chocolate cake? Either you allow yourself the occasional treat, or you try to find equally sophisticated puddings that are low in fat. You want, after all, to keep to your new way of eating. Although after seven years of healthy eating my taste-buds have learned to appreciate slightly different tastes, it has taken time and patience: much better to go slowly and stick to it than be too dramatic and too restrictive and then give it up. Begin by allowing yourself occasional treats: after six months you will not want them any more! The gentle and almost subversive route to health is a smooth path.

I do not try to cook to a target of a specific number of grams of fat per day. Cooking must remain an art and a joy; to bring science too far into the kitchen limits the pleasure of both cooking and eating. I hope you will find that your horizons are in fact extended by low-fat entertaining and that your enjoyment of food in the kitchen and at the table will be greater than before in the knowledge that you are eating well – in all senses.

Note on recipes

Ingredients in the recipes are given in both metric (g, ml, etc.) and imperial (oz, fl oz, etc.) measures. Use either set of quantities, but not a mixture of both, in any one recipe. All spoon measures are level spoons unless otherwise stated. Egg size, where not specified, is medium (size 3). Preparation and cooking times are given as a guideline: all timings are approximate.

The energy value for each recipe, rounded to the nearest 5 kilocalories and the nearest whole gram of fat, are based on the average serving given for each recipe.

PUMPKIN AND ORANGE SOUP

Preparation time: 15 minutes + 15 minutes cooking Serves 4

One serving has 55 kilocalories and negligible fat

- *750 g (1½ lb) skinned and pipped pumpkin flesh*
- *1 onion, chopped finely*
- *900 ml (1½ pints) water*
- *1 parsley stalk, bruised*
- *150 ml (¼ pint) fresh orange juice*
- *salt and freshly ground black pepper*

To serve:

- *natural yogurt*
- *chopped fresh mint*

A very simple, fairly traditional soup that is filling but not fattening. Pumpkins have a limited season so this can only be made in the late autumn and early winter.

Chop the pumpkin flesh into equal-sized cubes. Put them in a large saucepan with the onion, water, parsley stalk and pepper. Bring the liquid slowly up to the boil and let it simmer until the pumpkin is quite tender, about 15 minutes. Remove the parsley stalk.

Liquidise the soup. Pour it into a clean saucepan, reheat it and add the orange juice. Season it to taste.

To serve, pour the soup into warmed soup bowls. Marble it with a little yogurt and serve it sprinkled with chopped fresh mint.

CARROT AND ORANGE TIMBALES

Preparation time: 15 minutes + 45 minutes cooking — Serves 4

One serving has 90 kilocalories and 4 g fat

oil for greasing

375 g (12 oz) grated carrot

150 ml (¼ pint) orange juice

2 eggs, beaten

salt, pepper and nutmeg

Oven temperature:
Gas Mark 5/190°C/375°F

These are pretty and simple to make. They are delicious with either Tomato Vinaigrette (page 74) or Red Pepper Sauce (page 74).

Preheat the oven. Line the bases of four ramekin dishes or timbale moulds with circles of lightly greased, greaseproof paper. Simmer the grated carrot in the orange juice for 15 minutes. Allow the mixture to cool. Add the eggs and beat the mixture really well (do not whisk it). Season. Spoon the mixture into the dishes and smooth the tops.

Prepare a *bain-marie* (water bath): put the dishes in a shallow tin such as a roasting pan and carefully pour in boiling water to come two-thirds of the way up the dishes. Bring the water back to the boil on top of the stove and then transfer the *bain-marie* to the oven and bake the timbales for 30 minutes.

To serve: flood the bases of four side plates with either Tomato Vinaigrette or Red Pepper Sauce. Turn out the timbales, remove the greaseproof paper and put the timbales on top of the sauce. You can serve the timbales warm with the cold sauce, or chill them both, as you prefer.

LEEK AND SCALLOP SOUP

Preparation and cooking time: 45 minutes — Serves 4

One serving has 230 kilocalories and 1 g fat

- *1 kg (2 lb) leeks*
- *300 g (10 oz) potatoes, peeled and diced*
- *1.5 litres (2½ pints) chicken stock*
- *4 large scallops, cleaned*
- *salt and freshly ground black pepper*

This is a variation on the Vichyssoise theme. The scallop roes make a very pretty garnish for the soup.

Trim the leeks, wash them well and chop the white and pale green parts. Put them into a large saucepan with the potatoes and stock. Season well. Bring the stock up to the boil and let it simmer gently for 15 minutes.

Separate the roes from the main part of the scallops. Remove the muscle from the main part of the scallop and discard it. Add the whole scallops to the soup and simmer it for a further 4 minutes. Clean the roes and cut them in half horizontally.

Remove the soup from the heat and allow it to cool for a few minutes. Liquidise it well. Push it through a sieve into a clean saucepan and reheat it; taste it and adjust the seasoning. Add the roes to the soup and let it simmer for a further 3 minutes. To serve, ladle the soup into individual, warm soup bowls and allow two pieces of roe per head.

Leek and Scallop Soup

Plaice and Spinach Terrine

Carrot and Orange Timbales

PLAICE AND SPINACH TERRINE

Preparation time: 20 minutes + 30 minutes baking + several hours cooling

Serves 4

One serving has 180 kilocalories and 5 g fat

1 kg (2 lb) fresh spinach

1 large or 2 small plaice, skinned and filleted

a bunch of tarragon, chopped

3 tablespoons water

salt and freshly ground black pepper

Oven temperature:
Gas Mark 4/180°C/350°F

This is a very easy terrine to make, it requires no setting agent, and is simply an assembly job. It does not slice very well, so use a sharp, serrated-edged knife. This terrine is also delicious made with two chicken breasts that have been sliced in half horizontally, instead of the plaice.

Preheat the oven. Wash the spinach well and remove the stalks. Put it into a saucepan, cover the pan and cook the spinach for 4 minutes, shaking the pan regularly. Remove six large leaves. Refresh them under running cold water and leave them to drain on absorbent paper. Drain the remaining spinach well, pressing out all the water. Tip it on to a board and chop it roughly.

Use the reserved spinach leaves to line a 250 g (8 oz) non-stick loaf tin. Remember that the inside of the leaves should face the inside of the tin. Layer the chopped spinach and plaice fillets in the tin. Season with salt, pepper and tarragon as you go. Finish with a layer of spinach. Fold the whole spinach leaves over the chopped spinach.

Pour in the water. Cover the tin with wet greaseproof paper and place it in a *bain-marie* (see page 11 for how to prepare this). Bake it for 30 minutes. Leave the terrine to cool in the tin for a further 30 minutes.

Drain off the excess liquid. Leave the terrine to become completely cold. Turn it on to a wooden board and slice it. Serve slices with Carrot and Cardamom Sauce (page 72).

SPINACH ROULADE WITH SMOKED SALMON

Preparation time: 30 minutes + 2 hours cooling | Serves 4

One serving has 160 kilocalories and 7 g fat

500 g (1 lb) fresh spinach or 175 g (6 oz) frozen spinach, thawed

sunflower oil for greasing

2 eggs, separated

2 egg whites

a pinch of nutmeg

salt and freshly ground black pepper

For the filling:

175 g (6 oz) fromage frais

125 g (4 oz) smoked salmon, chopped

2 teaspoons chopped fresh dill

Oven temperature:
Gas Mark 5/190°C/375°F

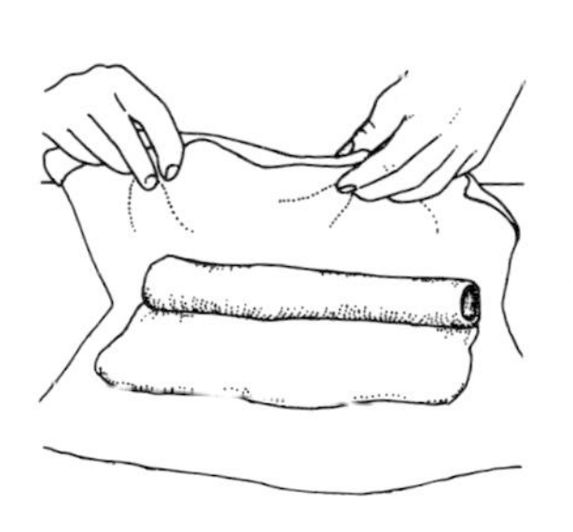

This looks very pretty if it is sliced and served on individual plates that have been flooded with Red Pepper Sauce (page 74).

Preheat the oven. Remove the stalks from the spinach leaves and wash them thoroughly. Cook the spinach in the water clinging to the leaves for 2–3 minutes until the leaves are limp, bright green and just cooked. Drain them thoroughly and chop them finely. If you are using frozen spinach, cook it according to the instructions on the packet.

Line a roasting tin with a double layer of greaseproof paper and brush the paper lightly with oil. Beat the egg yolks into the spinach and season it lightly with salt, pepper and nutmeg. Whisk the egg whites until they are stiff but not dry and fold them into the spinach. Pour this mixture into the roasting tin, spread it flat and bake it for 10–12 minutes.

Meanwhile, mix the filling ingredients together. When the roulade is cooked, turn it out on to a piece of greaseproof paper and remove the backing paper. Trim the edges with a sharp knife. Spread the filling over the roulade and roll it up as shown in the diagram. Leave the roulade to get cold before slicing it.

MEDITERRANEAN PRAWNS WITH SPRING ONION DIP

Preparation time: 15 minutes Serves 4

One serving has 130 kilocalories and 3 g fat

- *8 large Mediterranean prawns*
- *3 spring onions*
- *4 tablespoons greek yogurt*
- *salt and pepper*

Prawns are very low in fat and taste delicious. The dip is made from greek yogurt which is higher in fat than most natural yogurts; it is a luxury food, however, and this recipe is still much lower in fat than the sort of double cream and cream cheese dips which it imitates.

Shell the prawns but leave the heads on; make sure that you remove the coral, the tail and the black vein that runs the length of the back of the prawn.

Clean the spring onions, chop the white parts finely and mix them with the yogurt. Season to taste. Arrange the prawns on a large plate and put the dip in a bowl in the centre.

Mediterranean Prawns with Spring Onion Dip

PEA AND MINT SOUP

Preparation time: 10 minutes + 20 minutes cooking — Serves 4

One serving has 100 kilocalories and 1 g fat

500 g (1 lb) small frozen peas

1 onion, chopped finely

1 small potato, peeled and diced

12 mint leaves

1.2 litres (2 pints) chicken stock

salt and pepper

To serve:

greek yogurt

very finely chopped spring onion

I was on a train with my husband and said 'What is your favourite soup?' Looking surprised, he replied 'Pea soup'. Oh dear, I thought, how dull, but as he is my most handy recipe tester I thought that I would give his favourite soup a try. The result is, I think, utterly delicious.

Put the peas, onion, potato, mint leaves and chicken stock together in a saucepan; season, bring the liquid to the boil, cover the pan and let it simmer gently for 20 minutes.

Remove the soup from the heat, liquidise it very well and pour it through a sieve into a clean saucepan.

Reheat it for 1–2 minutes and pour it into a warmed soup tureen. Spoon on a dollop or two of greek yogurt and serve with a garnish of chopped spring onions.

DUCK BREAST AND PINE KERNEL SALAD

Preparation time: 20 minutes — Serves 4

One serving has 260 kilocalories and 20 g fat

3 handfuls of washed bitter salad leaves, such as lamb's lettuce and frisé lettuce

Hazelnut Oil French Dressing (page 71)

2 teaspoons sunflower oil

2 duck breasts, skinned and halved horizontally

50 g (2 oz) pine kernels

This can be served as either a first course or a supper dish.

Toss the salad leaves in the dressing and arrange them on four large plates. Heat the sunflower oil in a non-stick frying pan and in it cook the duck breast pieces for 2 minutes a side. Remove from the pan. Add the pine kernels and fry them until they are lightly browned. Slice the duck breasts and return them to the frying pan to reheat quickly. Scatter the duck breasts and pine kernels over the salad leaves and serve immediately.

MANGO AND LOBSTER SALAD

Preparation time: 25 minutes — Serves 4

One serving has 210 kilocalories and 9 g fat

4 handfuls of bitter salad leaves, such as frisé lettuce, lamb's lettuce, radicchio or oak leaf lettuce

French Dressing (page 70)

2 ripe mangoes

2 × 500 g (1 lb) cooked lobster

A wonderfully extravagant salad; the combination of mango and lobster is sensational. The dressing must be carefully blended so as to complement the salad without being overpowering. Rely on the flavour of the oil and use a minimal amount of seasoning.

Wash the salad leaves and dry them. Toss them in some of the French Dressing and arrange them on four plates.

Cut a thick slice from each side of the mangoes (diagram 1). Carefully peel off the skin and slice the flesh horizontally.

Cut the heads off the lobsters (diagram 2), pull off the claws and remove the shell, rather as if you were peeling a large prawn (diagram 3). Cut the body flesh (that is, the tail) into neat slices. Crack the claws but leave them whole. Arrange alternate slices of lobster and mango on each plate. Pour over the remaining dressing and garnish each with a claw.

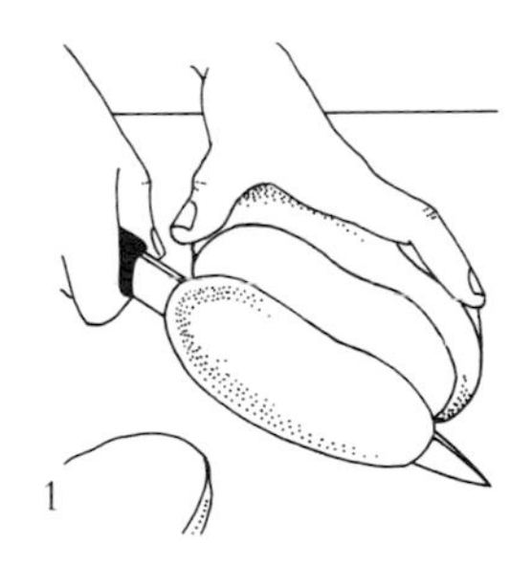

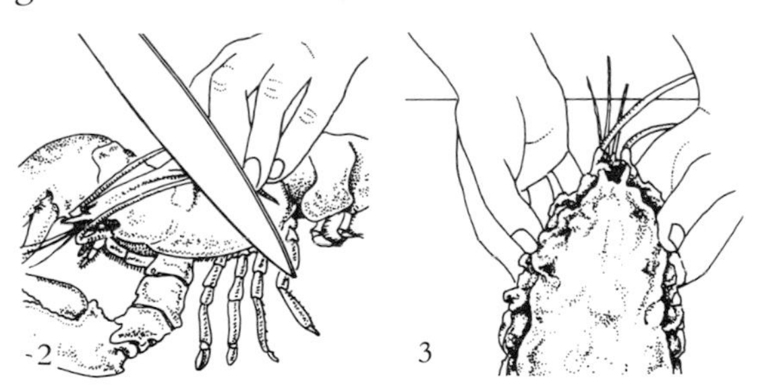

SMOKED SALMON, PASTA AND DILL SALAD

Preparation and cooking time: 20 minutes — Serves 4

One serving has 270 kilocalories and 8 g fat

175 g (6 oz) fresh 'paglia e fieno' or 175 g (6 oz) dried pasta spirals

175 g (6 oz) smoked salmon, cut in strips

1 tablespoon chopped fresh dill

French Dressing (page 70)

To decorate:

4 sprigs of fresh dill

One of the most encouraging things about the switch from conventional to healthy eating is that pasta is now classed as a 'good thing'. This luxurious pasta salad makes you feel you are eating an extravagant first course without indulging in anything other than healthy food.

Cook the pasta in plenty of boiling, salted water to which a tablespoon of oil has been added to prevent the pasta from sticking together. When the pasta is tender (about 5 minutes if fresh or 10–15 minutes if dried) drain it well, rinse it with boiling water and leave it to stand, turning it occasionally. Mix the pasta with the remaining ingredients. Serve on individual plates, decorating each plate with a sprig of fresh dill.

Smoked Salmon, Pasta and Dill Salad

Mango and Lobster Salad

Vegetable Terrine

VEGETABLE TERRINE

Preparation time: 1 hour + several hours setting Serves 4

One serving has 230 kilocalories and 15 g fat

10 large fresh spinach leaves

550 g (1 lb 2 oz) large carrots

grated rind and juice of ½ a lemon

6 small turnips

4 tablespoons water

25 g (1 oz) or 2 envelopes of gelatine

1 large ripe avocado

salt and pepper

This is a pretty, layered terrine. I have used carrots, turnips and avocados as the colours are so good but many combinations would work. Simply cook the vegetables to a purée, set them with gelatine and arrange them in layers as in the recipe.

It seems a shame to overcook the vegetables but for this recipe they do need to be absolutely soft. The trick is to cook them in the minimum amount of water, so that there is no need to drain off the excess. In this way there is less loss of minerals and vitamins in discarded water.

Wash the spinach very well and remove the tough stalks. Put it into a saucepan, without any extra water; cover and cook the spinach for 3 minutes. Remove the leaves, refresh them in cold water and leave them to drain on absorbent paper. Use the leaves (pretty-side outside) to line a non-stick 1 kg (2 lb) loaf tin.

Peel the carrots, slice them and cook them in the minimum quantity of water. When they are completely tender, drain and process them until they are absolutely smooth. Season the carrots and add the lemon rind.

Peel the turnips, slice them and cook them in the minimum quantity of water. When they are completely tender, drain them well and process until they are absolutely smooth. Season.

Put 4 tablespoons of water into a small saucepan, sprinkle on the gelatine and set it aside for 5 minutes to become spongy. Dissolve the gelatine over a gentle heat; when it is clear and warm stir two-thirds of it into the carrot purée and the remaining third into the turnip purée.

Spoon half the carrot purée into the loaf tin, smooth it down, cover the tin and leave it to set in the refrigerator.

Peel and slice the avocado, sprinkle it with lemon juice and arrange half of it on top of the carrot purée. Cover it carefully with the turnip purée, smooth the purée down and leave the terrine to set in the refrigerator.

Arrange the rest of the avocado on top of the turnip. Cover it with the remaining carrot purée, smooth the top down and refrigerate the terrine again.

To serve: place a large plate over the loaf tin. Turn the tin and plate over together. Remove the tin and slice the terrine with a serrated-edged knife.

MARINATED SALMON AND MELON SALAD

Preparation time: 4 hours marinating + 15 minutes — Serves 6

One serving has 170 kilocalories and 11 g fat

375 g (12 oz) piece of filleted and skinned fresh salmon

juice of 2 limes

18 green peppercorns

2 handfuls of bitter salad leaves, such as lamb's, frisé and oak leaf lettuce

1 small, ripe canteloupe or honeydew melon

French Dressing (page 70)

salt and pepper

A simple, light and refreshing first course.

Slice the salmon finely and marinate it for 4 hours in the lime juice and green peppercorns. Turn it occasionally. Wash and dry the salad leaves. Cut the melon in half and scoop out the seeds. Cut it into quarters, cut off the skin and slice the flesh finely. Toss the salad leaves in the dressing, arrange them on six small plates and cover the leaves with salmon and melon slices. Season well with salt and pepper.

TOMATO JELLY WITH FRESH MINT DRESSING

Preparation time: 30 minutes + 2 hours setting — Serves 4

One serving has 90 kilocalories and 6 g fat

- *550 g (1 lb 2 oz) canned tomatoes*
- *1 garlic clove, peeled*
- *1 bay leaf*
- *2 parsley stalks*
- *fresh basil (optional)*
- *6 peppercorns*
- *tomato juice*
- *3 tablespoons water*
- *15 g (½ oz) or 1 envelope of gelatine*
- *a squeeze of lemon juice*
- *salt, pepper and a little sugar*

To serve:

- *French Dressing (page 70) made with lots of chopped fresh mint*
- *fresh mint leaves*

This can make a very pretty summer first course as it is wonderfully light and refreshing. If you like, make it in individual moulds and serve them on small plates flooded with the dressing. This is not ideal for an outdoor buffet party as the jelly might melt in the sun (if the sun does come out) but it does look very pretty as part of an arrangement of party food.

Put the tomatoes, garlic, bay leaf, parsley stalks, basil, if using it, and peppercorns into a heavy saucepan with a little salt, pepper and sugar. Simmer the mixture gently for 15 minutes.

Strain and sieve the mixture into a measuring jug. Make it up to 450 ml (¾ pint) with tomato juice. Taste it and season well; then leave it to cool.

Put the water in a small saucepan and sprinkle over the gelatine. Leave it for 5 minutes to become spongy. Meanwhile, wet a 600 ml (1 pint) ring mould.

Dissolve the gelatine over a gentle heat until it is clear and warm. Stir it into the tomato mixture, add a squeeze of lemon juice and pour everything into the wetted mould. Leave the jelly in the refrigerator to set for at least 2 hours.

To turn out the jelly, dip the bottom of the mould briefly into hot water, put a round plate over the jelly and turn the plate and jelly over together so that the jelly falls out on to the plate. Pour the dressing into the centre of the mould and decorate the sides of the jelly with fresh mint leaves.

Tomato Jelly with Fresh Mint Dressing
Smoked Trout Pâté
Vegetable 'Pasta'

SMOKED TROUT PÂTÉ

Preparation time: 15 minutes + 3 hours chilling Serves 4

One serving has 220 kilocalories and 6 g fat

- *2 large smoked trout, skinned and boned*
- *375 g (12 oz) low-fat cottage cheese, sieved*
- *1 teaspoon grated fresh horseradish*
- *1 tablespoon lemon juice*
- *75 g (3 oz) sliced smoked salmon, cut in strips*
- *1 lime, sliced*
- *freshly ground black pepper*

This is a simple, attractive and sophisticated first course that can be made, but not decorated, in advance. It can either be served as described here or on individual plates, garnished with a sprig of herbs.

Pound together in a food processor the trout, cottage cheese, horseradish and lemon juice. If you do not have a food processor, chop the trout finely and beat it well with the other ingredients. Taste the mixture and season with black pepper. Pile the pâté into a pudding basin, cover it and refrigerate the pâté for 3 hours.

Turn the pâté out on to a dessert plate, arrange the strips of smoked salmon over the pâté and decorate it with slices of lime.

VEGETABLE 'PASTA'

Preparation time: 15 minutes + 2 hours chilling Serves 4

One serving has 75 kilocalories and 6 g fat

- *4 carrots*
- *4 medium-size courgettes*
- *French Dressing (page 70)*
- *1 tablespoon chopped fresh chives*

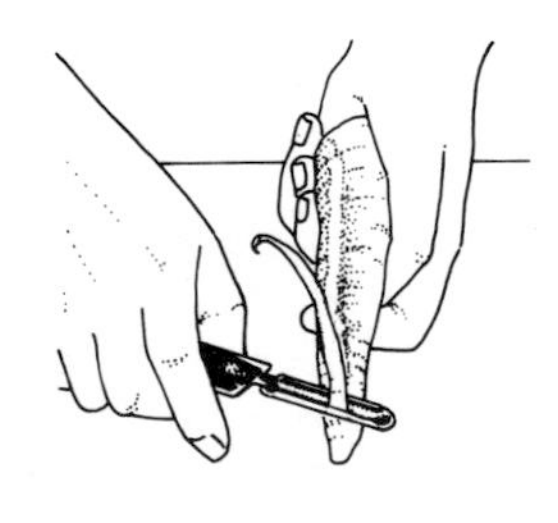

This recipe actually has no pasta in it at all! It is simply that the way the vegetables are prepared makes them look like pasta ribbons. This can be made well in advance and looks very pretty. It is a particularly good summer first course.

Peel the carrots. Using a swivel peeler, shred the carrots into long, thin ribbons as shown in the drawing. Top and tail the courgettes and shred them into long, thin ribbons.

Toss the carrots and courgettes in the dressing at least 2 hours before the meal so that the vegetables begin to curl. To serve, arrange the ribbons on individual plates and garnish each serving with chives.

WARM SCALLOP SALAD

Preparation time: 10 minutes | Serves 4

One serving has 150 kilocalories and 7 g fat

8 fresh scallops

4 handfuls of bitter salad leaves, such as frisé lettuce, lamb's lettuce and radicchio

Hazelnut Oil French Dressing (page 71)

1 tablespoon lemon juice

I like this salad particularly, because the subtlety of scallops barely cooked in lemon juice is a refreshing change from the conventional recipes for scallops cooked in a rich creamy or buttery sauce.

Clean the scallops. Remove the muscular white frill found opposite the orange roe (diagram 1). Separate the roe from the body (diagram 2) and slice both in half horizontally (diagram 3).

Wash the salad leaves and dry them. Toss them in the dressing and arrange them on four plates.

Put the scallops in a pan with the lemon juice. Put on a well fitting lid. Gently shake and toss them over a moderate heat for 30 seconds or until they have lost their glassiness. Do not cook them all the way through. Tip the warm scallops over the salad leaves and serve immediately.

1

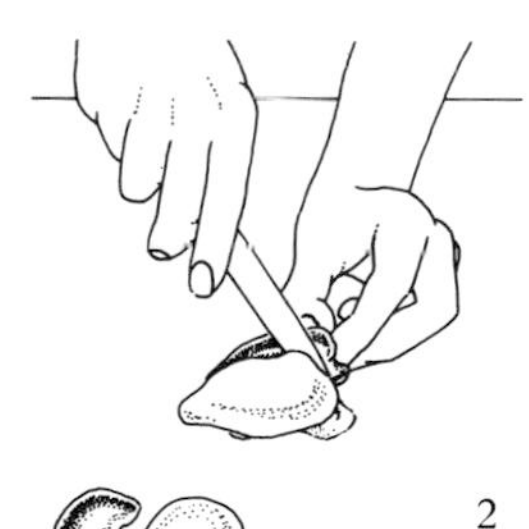

2

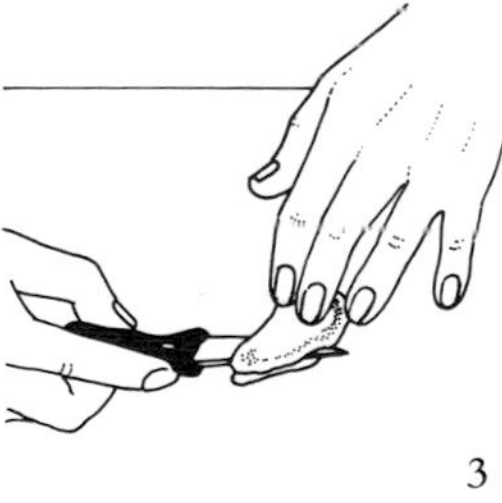

3

MAIN COURSES: FISH

SPICY FISH CURRY

Preparation and cooking time: 40 minutes — Serves 4

One serving has 250 kilocalories and 9 g fat

750 g (1½ lb) monkfish
sunflower oil
1 cm (½-inch) piece of fresh ginger, peeled and sliced
1 garlic clove, sliced
1 large onion, sliced
1 red pepper, de-seeded and cut in strips
1 green chilli, de-seeded and chopped
1 teaspoon ground cumin
1 teaspoon ground coriander
1 teaspoon ground cinnamon
1 teaspoon ground turmeric
water
125 g (4 oz) curd cheese
salt and pepper
To garnish:
roughly chopped fresh mint

Any firm white fish will do for this curry. It is fairly mild but it can be made hotter by using an extra green chilli. Be very careful not to overcook the fish as it will begin to fall apart and look unattractive.

Cut the monkfish into 2.5 cm (1-inch) cubes. Fry the cubes in a non-stick pan in a little sunflower oil with the ginger and garlic. Remove everything from the pan. Add the onion, pepper and green chilli and allow them to soften, without browning, for 2–3 minutes. Add the dry spices and cook for a further 2 minutes. Stir regularly and add a little extra oil if the spices are getting too dry or burnt.

Take the pan off the heat. Return the fish, ginger and garlic to it. Add enough water to half-cover the fish and vegetables and bring it gradually up to the boil. Season well. Let it simmer for 10 minutes.

Beat the cheese with a little water, add some of the hot fish juices, mix well and add the mixture to the pan. Bring the curry up to the boil but do not allow it to get too hot.

Pile the curry into a warm serving dish and serve it decorated with roughly chopped fresh mint.

Note: If you are not used to preparing green chillies, do this with great care as their juice can sting your eyes and mouth. Wear rubber gloves to handle them if you want and remove the seeds under running water.

Spicy Fish Curry

SALMON STEAKS WITH TOMATO AND BASIL

Preparation time: 40 minutes + 15–20 minutes cooking — Serves 4

One serving has 460 kilocalories and 31 g fat

4 × 175 g (6 oz) salmon steaks

10 tomatoes

1 onion, chopped

2 tablespoons water

2 tablespoons chopped fresh basil

50 g (2 oz) pine kernels

sunflower oil, plus extra for greasing

5 spring onions, chopped

salt and a little sugar

Oven temperature:
Gas Mark 4/180°C/350°F

I rather like being given a plate with a 'package' of food to unwrap, but if you prefer the parcels can be completely unwrapped and served on plates in the normal way.

Preheat the oven. Wipe the salmon steaks. Put each one on a fairly large, lightly oiled, round piece of tin foil.

Chop the tomatoes roughly. Put them into a large saucepan with the onion and water. Cook the mixture very slowly until quite a lot of water seeps out of the tomatoes. Increase the heat and let the sauce simmer for 15 minutes. Liquidise the sauce and push it through a sieve into a clean saucepan. Reduce it by rapid boiling to a thick consistency, let it cool slightly and add the basil with a little sugar and salt to taste.

Divide the tomato mixture between the salmon steaks, wrap them up and bake them in the oven for 15–20 minutes.

Meanwhile, cook the pine kernels in a little sunflower oil; be careful not to let them burn. Just before serving, open the parcels slightly and sprinkle each one first with pine kernels and then with the spring onions.

MONKFISH KEBABS WITH GINGER

Preparation and cooking time: 2 hours marinating + 20 minutes

Serves 4

One serving has 290 kilocalories and 2 g fat

1 kg (2 lb) monkfish

2.5 cm (1-inch) piece of root ginger

juice of ½ a lemon

3 medium-size red peppers

1 large onion

I am very fond of monkfish (or 'angler' as it is sometimes called, being such a greedy fish) because its texture is so good and so firm. This recipe is an ideal one for a barbecue. The fish does not really need cooking as the lemon juice will 'cook' it, it simply needs heating up.

Cut the monkfish into 2.5 cm (1-inch) cubes. Peel and slice the ginger thinly and marinate the monkfish in it, with the lemon juice, for 2 hours.

Remove the seeds and core from the red peppers; cut the flesh into 2.5 cm (1-inch) square pieces. Peel the onion, separate the layers and cut them into 2.5 cm (1-inch) square pieces. Blanch the peppers and onion together for 2 minutes. Refresh them in running cold water.

Heat the grill to its highest temperature. Skewer the monkfish cubes alternately with the red pepper and onion pieces on four skewers. Grill the kebabs for 6 minutes, turning the skewers every 2 minutes. Serve the kebabs on a bed of rice with Yogurt Sauce (page 71) if you like.

RED MULLET IN VINE LEAVES

Preparation and cooking time: 15 minutes | Serves 4

One serving has 460 kilocalories and 15 g fat

4 large red mullet, filleted

4 large fresh or preserved vine leaves

chopped fresh dill

salt, pepper and lemon juice

To serve:

lemon wedges

4 sprigs of dill

Ideally this recipe is for barbecues but it works very well done on a conventional domestic grill.

Remove any bones from the fish. Blanch the vine leaves in boiling water for 4 minutes. Refresh them under running cold water and leave to drain. Heat the grill to a moderate temperature. Season the fish with salt, pepper and lemon juice and sandwich the fillets (skin-side outwards) with fresh dill. Wrap each fish in a vine leaf and grill them for 3–4 minutes a side. Serve the fish on a warm plate and garnish with lemon wedges and a sprig of dill.

Red Mullet in Vine Leaves

Salmon Steaks with Tomato and Basil

Monkfish Kebabs with Ginger

TURBOT STEAKS EN PAPILLOTE WITH FRESH THYME

Preparation time: 20 minutes + 10 minutes cooking — Serves 4

One serving has 120 kilocalories and 2 g fat

1 tablespoon very finely shredded white of leek

1 tablespoon very finely shredded carrot

50 g (2 oz) tiny button mushrooms, sliced finely

sunflower oil for greasing

4 × 125 g (4 oz) turbot steaks

2 teaspoons fresh thyme leaves

lemon juice

150 ml (1/4 pint) dry white wine

salt and freshly ground black pepper

Oven temperature:
Gas Mark 7/220°C/425°F

Preheat the oven. Blanch the leek, carrot and mushrooms in boiling water for 1 minute. Refresh them in cold water and drain them well.

Cut four 40 cm (16-inch) diameter circles of greaseproof paper. Brush the circles very lightly with oil and place a turbot steak on one half of each round (diagram 1). Divide the vegetables, thyme, lemon juice and wine between the four steaks. Season them well. Fold the free half of the *papillote* paper over to make a parcel rather like an apple turnover. Fold the edges of the two layers of paper over twice together, twisting them and pressing hard to make an airtight seal (diagram 2).

Lightly brush two baking sheets with oil and put two *papillotes* on each sheet. Bake them for 10 minutes. Serve them *en papillote*, that is, each diner unwraps his or her own parcel on the plate.

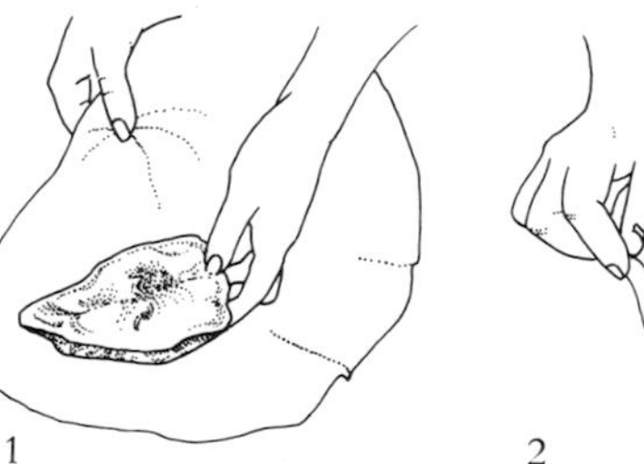

1

2

FILLET OF TROUT NIÇOISE WITH HAZELNUT DRESSING

Preparation and cooking time: 40 minutes Serves 4

One serving has 340 kilocalories and 17 g fat

- *4 large fillets of pink trout*
- *grapeseed oil*
- *lime juice*
- *125 g (4 oz) french beans*
- *1 small cauliflower*
- *4 tomatoes*
- *12 black olives, stoned*
- *Hazelnut Oil French Dressing (page 71)*
- *freshly ground black pepper*

Your aim when making this recipe is to serve the fish warm and the salad ingredients at room temperature; it can also be served cold, however, but the advantage of serving salads warm is that you get a clearer perception of their taste.

Brush the trout fillets with a little oil, season them with black pepper and lime juice and leave them to marinate while preparing the salad ingredients.

Top and tail the french beans. Blanch them for 2 minutes in boiling water. Refresh them under running cold water and drain them well. Break the cauliflower into florets. Blanch these for 3 minutes in boiling water. Refresh them under running cold water and drain them well. Prick the tomatoes and place them in boiling water for 15 seconds. Remove and skin them. Cut them into slivers, discarding the seeds.

Preheat the grill. Arrange the beans, cauliflower, tomatoes and olives on a serving dish or on individual plates. Leave a space for the fish. Pour over most of the dressing.

Grill the trout fillets until they are just cooked; I usually leave the skin on and grill them from the top for about 4 minutes. Whilst the trout is grilling, heat several meat skewers until they are very hot and use them to score a lattice pattern on each fillet. You won't need to do this if you are cooking on a charcoal grill.

Arrange the fillets on the plate or plates and pour the remaining dressing over them.

SEA-BASS WITH WILD RICE

Preparation time: soaking overnight + 40 minutes + 50 minutes cooking — Serves 4

One serving has 570 kilocalories and 25 g fat

1.25 kg (3 lb) sea-bass, cleaned and scaled
lemon juice
50 g (2 oz) brown rice, soaked overnight
50 g (2 oz) wild rice
25 g (1 oz) pine kernels
25 g (1 oz) sultanas
1 tablespoon chopped fresh dill
oil for greasing
1 onion, sliced
1 bay leaf
2 tablespoons white wine
freshly ground black pepper

To garnish:
a bunch of watercress

Oven temperature:
Gas Mark 4/180°C/350°F

Sally Procter, my co-principal at Leith's School of Food and Wine has also become very interested in healthy eating and this is one of her recipes. It is delicious made entirely with wild rice.

Preheat the oven. Season the inside of the sea-bass with a little lemon juice and black pepper. Wash both the rices very well and cook them for 30 minutes in plenty of boiling water. Drain and rinse them under cold water until they are completely cold. Drain them well. Add the pine kernels, sultanas and dill. Season to taste.

Put the sea-bass on a sheet of lightly oiled tin foil; stuff the gut cavity with the rice mixture. Scatter the onion over the sea-bass, and add the bay leaf and sprinkle the wine over the top. Draw the tin foil up to make a parcel.

Place the parcel on a large baking sheet and cook it in the preheated oven for 40–50 minutes. Serve this fish hot or cold, garnished with watercress.

Fillet of Trout Niçoise with Hazelnut Dressing
Sea-bass with Wild Rice

MAIN COURSES: MEAT, POULTRY AND GAME

LAMB COLLOPS WITH ONION PURÉE

Preparation time: 25 minutes + 45 minutes cooking Serves 4

One serving has 290 kilocalories and 17 g fat

2 large best end necks of lamb

a small bunch of fresh mint, chopped

2 teaspoons grapeseed oil

salt and freshly ground black pepper

For the purée:

1 tablespoon extra virgin olive oil

4 medium-size onions, chopped finely

salt and pepper

To garnish:

a small bunch of watercress

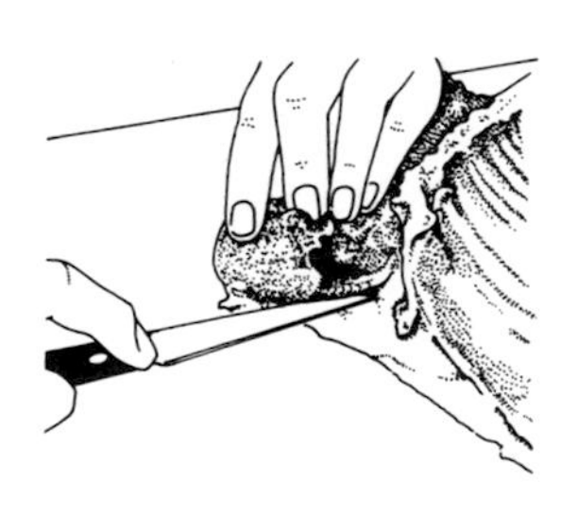

It may sound difficult to remove the eye of the meat but as long as the best ends have been 'chined' it is quite a simple operation. 'Chining' is a method of preparation in which the neck bones are sawn through by the 'eye' of the meat to make for easier home butchery.

With a small, sharp knife, carefully remove the eye of the best ends in one long piece, as in the diagram. Remove any fat or gristle and cut each into six neat collops or slices. Cover them with chopped mint, season well with freshly ground black pepper and leave the collops to marinate while you make the purée.

Heat the olive oil in a small saucepan. Add the onions, cover them with a piece of damp greaseproof paper and cook them very slowly until the onions are very soft. This may well take 45 minutes. Allow them to cool slightly. Liquidise the onions and push them through a sieve into a clean saucepan. Taste the purée and season it if necessary.

Heat the oil in a large, non-stick frying pan. Add the collops of lamb. Season them with a little salt and fry them gently for 1½ minutes a side. Place in a warmed serving dish and spoon a little warm purée on to each collop. Garnish with a bunch of watercress and serve immediately.

FILLET OF BEEF SALAD

Preparation and cooking time: 30 minutes — Serves 4

One serving has 190 kilocalories and 13 g fat

175 g (6 oz) fillet steak

Worcestershire sauce

1 small cauliflower

175 g (6 oz) broccoli

250 g (8 oz) cherry tomatoes

125 g (4 oz) french beans, topped and tailed

For the dressing:

3 tablespoons grapeseed oil

1 tablespoon good quality wine vinegar

1 teaspoon Dijon mustard

1 teaspoon grated fresh horseradish

1 garlic clove, crushed

1 tablespoon fresh chopped chives

This is an ideal summer party dish that is especially good for a buffet; it looks very attractive and is easy to eat with a fork.

Trim the fillet steak. Sprinkle it lightly with Worcestershire sauce. Dry-fry it in a non-stick frying pan for a total of six minutes. Leave it to get completely cold.

Cut the cauliflower and broccoli into florets. Cook them until they are half-tender in boiling water, about 5 minutes. Refresh them under running cold water and drain them well. Wash the tomatoes and remove the stalks. Cook the french beans for two minutes; refresh them under running cold water. Drain them well.

Mix together the ingredients for the dressing, except the chives, very well; use a tiny wire whisk if you have one. The salad can be prepared this far in advance but it should not be completed until a maximum of 30 minutes before serving.

Then cut the fillet steak into strips the size of your little finger; mix them with the cauliflower, broccoli, tomatoes and beans. Add the dressing and half the chives and stir gently. Pile into a serving dish and garnish the salad with the remaining chives.

BAKED PARTRIDGES WITH PORT AND GRAPES

Preparation time: 20 minutes + 40 minutes cooking — Serves 4

One serving has 410 kilocalories and 13 g fat

1 dessert apple

4 small oven-ready partridges

1 onion, chopped

450 ml (3/4 pint) water

1 tablespoon port

50 g (2 oz) seedless grapes

Oven temperature:
Gas Mark 5/[illegible]/375°F

Preheat the oven. Cut the apple into four and put a quarter inside each partridge. Put the chopped onion into the bottom of a roasting tin. Pour on the water. Put the partridges on a wire rack and place this on top of the roasting tin. Bake the partridges in the oven, basting them with water occasionally, for 40 minutes.

Remove the partridges from the oven. Tip the apple and any meat juices from the partridges into the roasting tin. Bring the liquid in the tin up to the boil and stir it vigorously to pulverise the apple. Push it through a sieve into a clean saucepan, pressing well to extract all the flavour. It should be the required syrupy consistency; if it is too thin, boil it rapidly to reduce it. Add the port and boil the sauce for 30 seconds; add the grapes and allow them to warm through. Serve the partridges on a warmed plate and either pour the sauce over or serve it separately.

Baked Partridges with Port and Grapes

Fillet of Beef Salad

Calves' Liver with Fresh Sage

CALVES' LIVER WITH FRESH SAGE

Preparation and cooking time: 30 minutes | Serves 4

One serving has 330 kilocalories and 16 g fat

- *750 g (1½ lb) calves' liver*
- *sunflower oil*
- *2 tablespoons chopped fresh sage*
- *150 ml (¼ pint) light stock*
- *125 ml (4 fl oz) red wine*
- *1 small onion, chopped*
- *salt and freshly ground black pepper*

Calves' liver is very high in cholesterol but very low in fat and high in iron. It tastes delicious but has to be treated with a little respect: cook it quickly and serve it immediately to prevent it from becoming tough.

Skin the liver, slice it as thinly as possible and remove any tubes. Lay it on the grill pan. Brush it lightly with oil, grind over plenty of black pepper and add a little of the fresh sage. Set the liver aside while you prepare the sauce.

Put the stock, wine and onion together in a small pan. Simmer the sauce over a gentle heat for 5 minutes. Increase the temperature, and by boiling it rapidly, reduce the sauce to half its original quantity. While the sauce is reducing, heat the grill. Grill the liver for 2 minutes a side; it should be brown on the outside and pink in the middle. Add the remaining sage to the sauce. Taste and season it as required.

Put the liver on a warm serving plate. Pour the sauce over and serve it immediately; the liver will toughen on standing.

QUAILS WITH CHESTNUTS, APPLES AND CALVADOS

Preparation time: 15 minutes + 35 minutes cooking — Serves 4

One serving has 460 kilocalories and 15 g fat

8 small quails

2 dessert apples, peeled, cored and sliced thickly

150 ml (1/4 pint) chicken stock

1 onion, sliced

1 bay leaf

1 parsley stalk, bruised

3 tablespoons calvados or brandy (optional)

140 g (5 oz) can of whole unsweetened chestnuts

freshly ground black pepper

To garnish:

chopped fresh chives

Oven temperature:
Gas Mark 6/200°C/400°F

This is a recipe that was developed by Sally Procter at Leith's School of Food and Wine. It is an excellent way to cook quails as they keep beautifully moist.

Preheat the oven. Season the quails with pepper and stuff them with a few slices of apple. Place them in a small roasting tin with the stock, onion, bay leaf, parsley stalk, calvados or brandy if using it and four of the chestnuts. Cover the tin with foil and roast the quails for 25 minutes. Remove the foil and roast them for a further 10 minutes or until they are tender, depending on their size. Remove the quails to a warm serving dish and keep them warm in the turned-off oven.

Strain the cooking liquor into a saucepan, pressing well to extract all the flavour. Skim off any fat and reduce it by rapid boiling to about 300 ml (1/2 pint).

Add the remaining apple slices and simmer them gently for 2 minutes; add the remaining chestnuts and simmer them for a further minute. Spoon the sauce, apples and chestnuts over the quails and scatter on the chopped chives. Serve any extra sauce separately.

LAMB WITH MUNG BEANS

Preparation time: 10 minutes + 4 hours soaking + 1½ hours cooking — Serves 4

One serving has 280 kilocalories and 7 g fat

250 g (8 oz) trimmed weight lean lamb, preferably leg

1 teaspoon sunflower oil

1 large onion, sliced

2 garlic cloves, sliced

1.2 litres (2 pints) beef stock

1 tablespoon tomato purée

1 tablespoon chopped fresh rosemary

250 g (8 oz) mung beans, soaked for 4 hours

5 cloves, tied together in a small piece of muslin

salt and freshly ground black pepper

Oven temperature:
Gas Mark 2/150°C/300°F

Preheat the oven. Cut the meat into 2.5 cm (1-inch) cubes. Fry the cubes in the oil, in a non-stick frying pan, until they are well browned all over. Transfer the meat to a flameproof casserole.

Fry the onion and garlic for 2 minutes. Add the stock, tomato purée, rosemary, salt and pepper. Bring the liquid up to the boil, season it to taste and pour it over the meat. Drain the beans, rinse them and add them to the casserole. Bring the casserole up to the boil, add the little bag of cloves, cover it and transfer it to the oven. Bake the casserole for 1½ hours.

POT AU FEU

Preparation time: 20 minutes + 3 hours cooking — Serves 4

One serving has 240 kilocalories and 5 g fat

a piece of topside weighing about 500 g (1 lb)

1 kg (2 lb) broken beef bones

pared rind of 1 orange

2.25 litres (4 pints) water

500 g (1 lb) carrots, peeled and sliced thickly

125 g (4 oz) turnips, peeled and sliced thickly

To make a perfect Pot au Feu you really need the slow oven of a solid fuel cooker. The secret of success is fantastically slow cooking which makes for a clear broth.

Trim the meat of all visible fat and tie it into a compact shape with string. Put the bones and orange rind into the bottom of a very large saucepan. Add the meat and three-quarters of the water, with a pinch of salt. Bring the liquid slowly up to the boil, skimming it constantly.

500 g (1 lb) leeks, sliced

a bulb of fennel, sliced

3 onions, peeled, 1 stuck with 8 cloves

2 sticks of celery, chopped

a pinch of salt

Simmer it for 2 minutes. Add the remaining cold water. Skim the liquid again when it returns to simmering point. Continue skimming until the scum is almost white. Then cook for one hour. Add the vegetables and continue to cook very, very slowly for about 1½ hours.

Traditionally, the stock is served as a soup and the meat and vegetables as a main course, with boiled potatoes.

SPICED BEEF

Preparation time: 25 minutes + 8 days marinating + 1½ hours cooking

Serves 4

One serving has 360 kilocalories and 12 g fat

1 large garlic clove, peeled

1.25 kg (3 lb) boneless sirloin of beef, tied

25 g (1 oz) soft brown sugar

25 g (1 oz) ground allspice

3 bay leaves, chopped

75 g (3 oz) salt

500 g (1 lb) plain flour

water

Oven temperature:
Gas Mark 5/190°C/375°F

Serve very thin slices of this delicious beef with a variety of salads and small baked potatoes for a traditional Boxing Day dinner. This recipe takes eight days to complete.

Cut the garlic into slivers. Trim the beef of any visible fat and stick the garlic slivers into it. Rub the surface of the joint with sugar. Leave it in a cool place for 12 hours.

Mix together the allspice, bay leaves and salt. Rub a little of this mixture all over the meat every day for the next week.

Preheat the oven. Make a thick, doughy paste by mixing together the flour and some water. Wrap it all around the beef. Put the beef into a roasting pan, pour in a small cup of water and bake for 1½ hours.

Remove the beef from the oven and leave it to cool in the pastry case. Snip off the crust and discard it before serving the beef.

BRAISED VENISON

Preparation time: 20 minutes + 3 hours cooking — Serves 4

One serving has 560 kilocalories and 19 g fat

1 small saddle of venison

1 tablespoon sunflower oil

1 onion, sliced

2 carrots, sliced

1 parsnip, cut into chunks

3 sticks of celery, chopped

2 teaspoons plain flour

150 ml (1/4 pint) red wine

150 ml (1/4 pint) beef stock, plus extra if necessary

1 bay leaf

a sprig of fresh thyme

salt and freshly ground black pepper

To garnish:

a small bunch of watercress

Oven temperature:
Gas Mark 3/170°C/325°F

Preheat the oven. Trim away as much fat, sinew and tough membrane as you can from the venison. Heat the oil in a large flameproof casserole dish and brown the venison well on all sides. Remove it from the casserole. Add the onion, carrots, parsnip and celery and cook them slowly for 5 minutes. Add the flour and cook it for a further minute. Remove the casserole from the heat and add the wine and beef stock. Return the casserole to the heat and bring it gradually up to the boil, stirring continually. Reduce the heat and return the venison to the casserole. Season it well and add the bay leaf and thyme.

Cover the casserole tightly and put it in the oven for 2½–3 hours. Check it every so often and add a little extra stock or water if the casserole is drying out.

When the venison is cooked, remove it and place it on a warm serving dish. Strain the liquid from the vegetables into a saucepan. Apply a *little* pressure to the vegetables to push a little of the pulp through but discard the rest of the vegetables. Check the consistency of the gravy: if it is too thick, add a little water or stock; if it is too thin, boil it rapidly to reduce it. Taste it and season it as required.

To serve, lift the loins off the saddle and carve the meat into neat collops or slices. Pour a little of the gravy over the meat and garnish it with the bunch of watercress. Serve the remaining gravy separately in a warmed sauceboat.

CHICKEN CURRY

Preparation time: 20 minutes + 45 minutes cooking | Serves 4

One serving has 350 kilocalories and 11 g fat

1 chicken, skinned and jointed into 8 pieces

sunflower oil

2 teaspoons ground turmeric

1/4 teaspoon ground ginger

seeds of 4 cardamom pods, crushed

1/4 teaspoon ground cinnamon

1/4 teaspoon chilli powder (cayenne)

chicken stock

1 garlic clove, crushed

1 green chilli, de-seeded and chopped

2 onions, sliced

4 leeks, sliced

2 tablespoons natural yogurt

salt and pepper

To garnish:

roughly chopped fresh coriander

Recipes for curries are legion. This is a simple, fairly mild one but if you prefer a hotter curry, add extra green chillies. If leeks are not in season, use extra onions.

I made this quite recently using boned, skinned chicken breasts. It was delicious and only took 25 minutes to cook.

Fry the chicken joints in a non-stick saucepan using a minimal amount of oil. Sprinkle them with the turmeric, ginger, cardamom seeds, cinnamon and chilli powder. Fry them for a further minute, cover the pan and leave the chicken to marinate while you prepare the other ingredients, or for at least 10 minutes.

Add enough chicken stock to come a third of the way up the chicken. Bring it to the boil. Add the garlic, chilli, onions and leeks. Cover the pan and let it simmer, without removing the lid, for 45 minutes.

Remove the chicken joints and vegetables to a warm dish with a slotted spoon; cover the dish. Reduce the sauce a little by boiling it rapidly. Remove the sauce from the heat, cool it for a minute or two, taste it, season and whisk in the yogurt. Pour the sauce over the chicken; serve garnished with the chopped coriander.

Note: If preferred, this can be baked at Gas Mark 4/180°C/350°F for 1 hour.

PIGEON BREASTS WITH SOY SAUCE AND CHILLIES

Preparation and cooking time: 30 minutes marinating + 10 minutes — Serves 4

One serving has 390 kilocalories and 22 g fat

8 pigeon breasts, skinned

2 fresh green chillies, de-seeded and chopped roughly

4 tablespoons soy sauce

To garnish:

a small bunch of watercress

Pigeons are very low in fat and therefore a good meat to eat. I have never been keen on them, however, as they can be dry and tough and seem rather a bore to eat. This recipe solves the problem as only the breasts are used: pigeon legs and wings are proportionally tiny so you can happily put them into the stock pot; breasts can then be cooked rather like a steak and served moist and rare. Soy sauce is high in salt so do not use more than the quantity recommended here.

Put the pigeon breasts, chillies and soy sauce together in a bowl. Mix them well, cover the bowl and leave the breasts to marinate for 30 minutes.

Heat the grill to a medium heat. When it is hot, grill the pigeon breasts for 3 minutes a side and serve immediately on a bed of rice. Pour over any pan juices and garnish the dish with watercress.

Pigeon Breasts with Soy Sauce and Chillies
Stir-fried Chicken with Cashews
Chicken Breasts with Ginger

STIR-FRIED CHICKEN WITH CASHEWS

Preparation and cooking time: 20 minutes | Serves 4

One serving has 270 kilocalories and 14 g fat

500 g (1 lb) boneless, skinless chicken

2.5 cm (1-inch) piece of fresh ginger, peeled and sliced

2 small garlic cloves, peeled and sliced

2 teaspoons cornflour

1 tablespoon soy sauce

1 tablespoon dry sherry

150 ml (¼ pint) chicken stock

1 tablespoon sunflower or grapeseed oil

50 g (2 oz) unsalted shelled cashew nuts

salt and pepper

To garnish:

2 spring onions, chopped

Trim the chicken of all fat and cut it into even-sized pieces. Put the pieces in a bowl with the ginger and garlic; cover the bowl and leave it to stand. Mix the cornflour with the soy sauce, sherry and chicken stock. Set this aside.

Heat the oil in a wok or a large frying pan. Add the cashew nuts and stir-fry them until they are lightly browned. Remove them with a slotted spoon. Add the chicken with the ginger and garlic and stir-fry until the chicken is cooked and tender. This will take 4–5 minutes. Add the liquid ingredients and stir until they are well blended and the liquid has thickened. Add a little water if it seems too thick. Taste the sauce and season it if necessary. Pile everything into a warmed serving dish and sprinkle over the spring onions and cashew nuts.

CHICKEN BREASTS WITH GINGER

Preparation time: 15 minutes + at least 30 minutes marinating + 30 minutes cooking Serves 4

One serving has 170 kilocalories and 4 g fat

4 chicken breasts, boned and skinned

1 small onion, chopped finely

2 garlic cloves, peeled and sliced

1 cm (½-inch) piece of fresh ginger, peeled and chopped

2 tablespoons soy sauce

1 tablespoon dry sherry

the seeds of 5 green cardamom pods

2 teaspoons concentrated apple juice (or clear honey if not available)

Oven temperature:
Gas Mark 4/180°C/350°F

This is my stand-by recipe, which is quick and easy to make and always popular. The longer the chicken breasts are marinated the better they taste once cooked, but just half an hour in the marinade will give them an excellent flavour.

Preheat the oven. Remove any fat from the chicken breasts. Mix together the onion, garlic, ginger, soy sauce, sherry, cardamom seeds and apple juice or honey in a bowl. Add the chicken breasts, turn them well, cover the bowl and marinate for anything between 30 minutes and 24 hours.

Arrange a large sheet of kitchen foil in a flat baking dish and place the chicken breasts on top, making sure that they do not touch each other (diagram 1). Pour over the marinade and fold the foil back over the chicken. Seal the edges tightly, but leave room for a little circulation of air inside the parcel (diagram 2). Bake the chicken for 30 minutes. Serve the breasts with the marinade as a sauce.

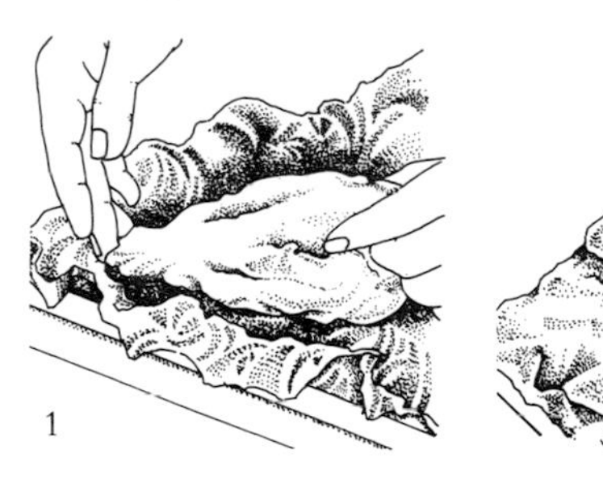

GUINEA-FOWL BRAISED WITH CARAMEL AND ORANGES

Preparation time: 10 minutes + 1½ hours cooking | Serves 4

One serving has 290 kilocalories and 10 g fat

2 guinea-fowl

2 teaspoons sunflower oil

50 g (2 oz) shallots, chopped finely

25 g (1 oz) granulated sugar

1 tablespoon wine vinegar

175 ml (6 fl oz) chicken stock

juice of 2 oranges, strained

salt and freshly ground black pepper

To garnish:

1 orange

a small bunch of watercress

Oven temperature:
Gas Mark 5/190°C/375°F

A guinea-fowl is rather like a small but perfectly flavoured chicken. It is low in fat and therefore the flesh can be dry if roasted, so it is better pot-roasted as in the following recipe.

Preheat the oven. Remove any feathers from the guinea-fowl and wipe their insides clean with a damp cloth. Heat the oil in a flameproof casserole. Add the guinea-fowl and brown them all over. Remove them from the casserole.

Reduce the heat and add the shallots; cook them for 2 minutes. Add the sugar and vinegar, dissolve the sugar over a gentle heat and then boil the liquid until the sugar caramelises. Pour on the stock – it will hiss and splutter so take care – and stir over a gentle heat, until the caramel lumps disappear. Add the orange juice. Season well with salt and pepper. Return the guinea-fowl to the casserole and bring the cooking liquor up to the boil. Cover the casserole and pot-roast it for 1½ hours.

Remove the guinea-fowl and joint them as you would a chicken. Arrange the pieces on a warmed serving plate. Skim as much fat as possible from the cooking liquor. Strain it into a clean saucepan, skim it again and boil it rapidly for 3 minutes.

Garnish the guinea-fowl with segments of orange and a small bunch of watercress and serve the hot sauce separately.

STIR-FRIED BEEF WITH SZECHWAN PEPPERCORNS

Preparation time: 20 minutes + 45 minutes marinating + 10 minutes frying

Serves 4

One serving has 180 kilocalories and 9 g fat

250 g (8 oz) very lean tender beef, such as fillet or rump

175 g (6 oz) carrots, peeled and cut into julienne strips

5 sticks of celery, trimmed and cut into julienne strips

2 teaspoons cornflour

1 teaspoon concentrated apple juice

4 tablespoons water

2 teaspoons sunflower oil

2 dried red chillies, de-seeded and chopped

½ teaspoon Szechwan peppercorns

sesame oil

For the marinade:

2 tablespoons soy sauce

1 teaspoon concentrated apple juice

1 tablespoon Shaoshing wine or sherry

1 teaspoon sesame oil

½ teaspoon ground roasted Szechwan peppercorns

To garnish:

chopped fresh coriander

This recipe is a healthy version of the classic Szechwan dry-fried beef, although it is not so crispy, as the beef is stir-fried rather than deep-fried. It is a very spicy dish, so serve it with plenty of boiled rice. Shaoshing wine is a Chinese wine; our nearest equivalent is dry sherry. Szechwan peppercorns are very strong peppercorns. They can be frozen very successfully.

Cut the beef into shreds the length of your little finger. Mix together the ingredients for the marinade and add the beef. Leave to marinate for 45 minutes. Soak the carrots and celery in a bowl of salted water for 45 minutes. Rinse them and pat them dry. Mix together 1 teaspoon cornflour, the concentrated apple juice and water.

Drain the beef of its marinade (reserve the marinade) and mix the beef with the remaining cornflour. Heat the sunflower oil in a wok or large frying pan and stir-fry the beef over a high heat. Remove it from the pan and set it aside. Stir-fry the chillies, carrots and celery for 2–3 minutes. Add the beef, cook it for a further minute and gradually add the marinade and the cornflour mixture. Sprinkle on the Szechwan peppercorns and a little sesame oil. Pile everything into a warm serving dish and sprinkle it with the fresh coriander.

LAMB KEBABS WITH SATÉ SAUCE

Preparation time: 15 minutes + 1 hour marinating + 10 minutes grilling

Serves 4

One serving has 250 kilocalories and 16 g fat

For the marinade:

1 medium-size onion, chopped finely

1 garlic clove, crushed

1 teaspoon ground coriander

1 teaspoon ground ginger

3 tablespoons soy sauce

juice of 1 lemon

1 teaspoon concentrated apple juice

ground black pepper

For the kebabs:

375 g (12 oz) leg lamb, well trimmed and cut in 2.5 cm (1-inch) cubes

1 large green pepper, de-seeded and cut into 8

1 large onion, cut into 8

grapeseed oil

For the saté sauce:

1 small onion, chopped finely

2 teaspoons oil

½ teaspoon chilli powder

25 g (1 oz) crunchy peanut butter

1 tablespoon soy sauce

2 teaspoons lemon juice

150 ml (¼ pint) cold water

concentrated apple juice

salt to taste

Mix together the ingredients for the marinade, add the meat and leave for 1 hour.

Meanwhile, make the sauce. Cook the onion in the oil until it is just beginning to soften. Add the chilli powder and cook it for a few seconds. Remove the pan from the heat, add the peanut butter, soy sauce, lemon juice and water. Return the pan to the heat and stir until the sauce is thick and smooth. Season it to taste with concentrated apple juice and salt.

Heat the grill. Skewer the meat alternately with the green pepper and onion on four skewers. Brush with a little oil and grill the kebabs for about 6 minutes, turning the skewers every 2 minutes. Serve immediately, as the meat toughens if it is kept for any length of time.

CHICKEN WITH BLACK BEAN SAUCE

Preparation and cooking time: 30 minutes marinating + 20 minutes

Serves 4

One serving has 290 kilocalories and 11 g fat

4 large chicken breasts, skinned and boned

2 tablespoons soy sauce

2 tablespoons fermented black beans

1 tablespoon sunflower oil

1 garlic clove, peeled and sliced

2.5 cm (1-inch) piece of fresh ginger, peeled and cut into slivers

2 level teaspoons cornflour

150 ml (¼ pint) water

1 tablespoon dry sherry

1 teaspoon concentrated apple juice

1 teaspoon sesame oil

3 spring onions, washed and sliced diagonally

In Chinese restaurants this would come under the heading of a 'sizzling dish'. I often choose dishes from that section because they sound so exciting. In fact, I think that they often cook the food in a fairly conventional way and then tip it on to a fantastically hot dish just before you get it! So the fact that this chicken doesn't actually sizzle is immaterial. Fermented black beans can be bought in cans or vacuum packs.

Remove any fat from the chicken breasts and cut them into bite-sized pieces. Leave the pieces to marinate in soy sauce for 30 minutes.

Meanwhile, make the black bean sauce. Wash the beans again and again; they are very salty. Heat the oil in a wok or large frying pan, add the garlic and ginger and stir-fry them for 1 minute. Add the chicken and stir-fry it for a further 2-3 minutes. Mix together the cornflour, water, sherry and apple juice. Add the beans and cornflour mixture to the wok. Stir-fry until the liquid is thickened and shiny. Add the sesame oil and two of the spring onions. Pile everything into a serving dish and garnish the dish with the remaining chopped spring onion.

BONED CHICKEN WITH LEEKS

Preparation time: 25 minutes + 1¼ hours cooking | Serves 6

One serving has 415 kilocalories and 30 g fat

1.5 kg (3 lb) chicken

6 leeks

1 large carrot

fresh mint leaves

125 g (4 oz) ricotta cheese

salt and freshly ground black pepper

Oven temperature:
Gas Mark 6/200°C/400°F

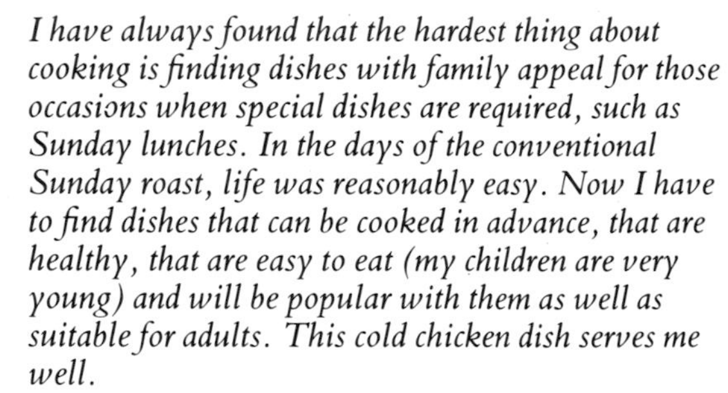

I have always found that the hardest thing about cooking is finding dishes with family appeal for those occasions when special dishes are required, such as Sunday lunches. In the days of the conventional Sunday roast, life was reasonably easy. Now I have to find dishes that can be cooked in advance, that are healthy, that are easy to eat (my children are very young) and will be popular with them as well as suitable for adults. This cold chicken dish serves me well.

The stuffing from this recipe can be cooked on its own and makes a very good terrine for a first course. It, too, can be served with the Red Pepper Sauce (page 74).

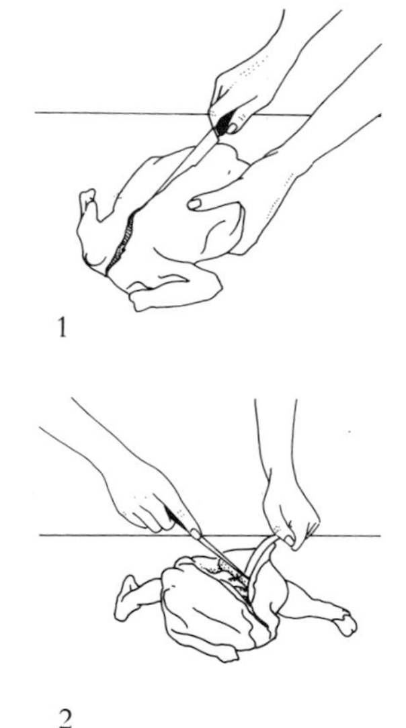

1

2

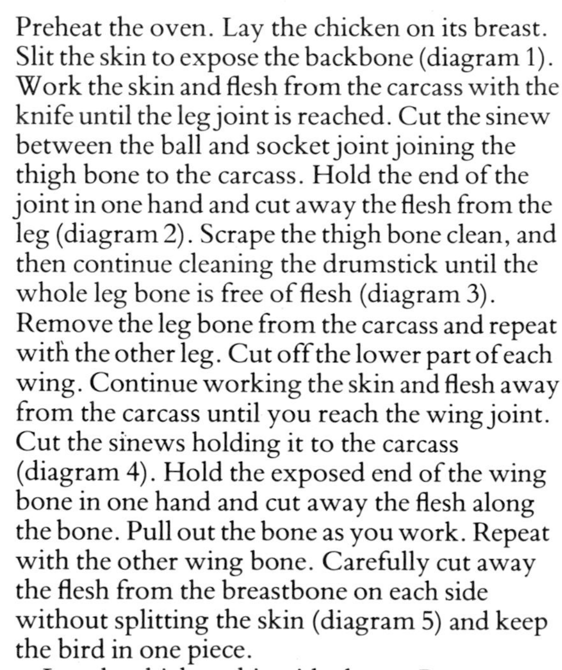

Preheat the oven. Lay the chicken on its breast. Slit the skin to expose the backbone (diagram 1). Work the skin and flesh from the carcass with the knife until the leg joint is reached. Cut the sinew between the ball and socket joint joining the thigh bone to the carcass. Hold the end of the joint in one hand and cut away the flesh from the leg (diagram 2). Scrape the thigh bone clean, and then continue cleaning the drumstick until the whole leg bone is free of flesh (diagram 3). Remove the leg bone from the carcass and repeat with the other leg. Cut off the lower part of each wing. Continue working the skin and flesh away from the carcass until you reach the wing joint. Cut the sinews holding it to the carcass (diagram 4). Hold the exposed end of the wing bone in one hand and cut away the flesh along the bone. Pull out the bone as you work. Repeat with the other wing bone. Carefully cut away the flesh from the breastbone on each side without splitting the skin (diagram 5) and keep the bird in one piece.

Lay the chicken skin-side down. Remove any

Boned Chicken with Leeks
Leek and Carrot Terrine

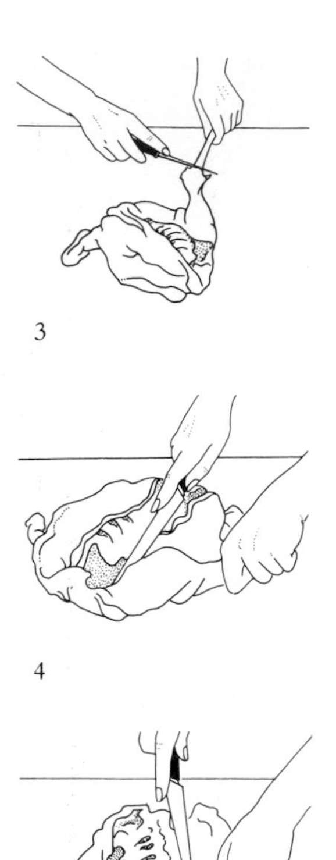
3

4

5

large pieces of fat and season it lightly. Cut the leeks in half lengthways and blanch them for 2 minutes in boiling water. Refresh them in running cold water and drain them well on absorbent paper. Peel the carrot. Discard the trimmings and then continue to peel the carrot into long, thin ribbons. Blanch these for 1 minute. Wash the mint leaves.

Layer the leeks, carrot ribbons, mint leaves and cheese in the centre of the chicken. Try to imagine how it will look when carved and make it look attractive. Season it lightly. Fold the sides of the chicken up to make a roll. Wrap the chicken in a damp piece of muslin or 'j' cloth. Tie the ends of the cloth together. Bake the chicken for 1¼ hours on a wire rack in a roasting tin. Unwrap it and leave to get completely cold.

Serve the chicken cut in slices and hand Red Pepper Sauce (page 74) separately, if you like.

Leek and Carrot Terrine: A pretty first course can be made by layering 8 small leeks, 1 large carrot, several fresh mint leaves and 125 g (4 oz) ricotta cheese, prepared as in the above recipe, in a small, non-stick loaf tin and baking it covered in a *bain marie* (water bath) for 35 minutes at Gas Mark 6/200°C/400°F. (See method for Carrot and Orange Timbales, page 11, for how to prepare a *bain marie.*) Leave to cool, cover the leeks with cling film and put some weights on top; anything can be used. If you have a second loaf tin, put it on top of the cling film and fill it with weights. When the terrine is cold, drain off any liquid, turn it out and slice it with a serrated-edged knife. Serve with Red Pepper Sauce (page 74).

CHICKEN BREASTS WITH RED PEPPER SAUCE

Preparation and cooking time: 30 minutes + 40 minutes for Red Pepper Sauce — Serves 4

One serving has 200 kilocalories and 8 g fat

4 chicken breasts, skinned and boned

3 tablespoons very finely shredded white of leek

2 tablespoons very finely shredded carrot

2 tablespoons chopped fresh mint

salt and freshly ground black pepper

To serve:

Red Pepper Sauce (page 74)

a few watercress leaves

Remove any fat from the chicken breasts. Mix the leek, carrot and mint together and season them. Put this stuffing between the main part of the breasts and the loose fillet. Wrap each breast in a piece of cling film. Poach the chicken breasts in water for 15 minutes.

Remove the breasts from the saucepan, unwrap them and leave them to become completely cold. Flood the base of four large plates with the Red Pepper Sauce. Put a chicken breast on each plate and garnish the plate with watercress leaves.

Note: If you don't want to cook with cling film the breasts can simply be cooked in chicken stock. The advantage of the cling film is that it keeps the chicken moist and in good shape and retains all its flavour.

CAULIFLOWER WITH GINGER AND SESAME SEEDS

Preparation time: 10 minutes + 30 minutes cooking   Serves 4

One serving has 85 kilocalories and 6 g fat

1 large cauliflower

2.5 cm (1-inch) piece of root ginger, peeled and chopped

1 tablespoon sunflower or grapeseed oil

water

1 rounded tablespoon sesame seeds

This recipe sounds extraordinary in that the cauliflower is cooked for 30 minutes; its deliciousness justifies it, however, as the cauliflower tastes wonderfully full of ginger at the end.

Break the cauliflower into florets. Cook the ginger in the oil for 1 minute. Add the cauliflower and a little water. Place the pan over a low heat and cook the cauliflower very slowly for 30 minutes. Check every so often that there is a little water in the bottom of the pan to prevent the cauliflower 'catching'.

When the cauliflower is nearly cooked, heat the sesame seeds in a saucepan. As soon as they begin to pop (about 1 minute) cover the pan with a lid to stop them jumping out of the pan and shake the pan for about 30 seconds. Mix together the cauliflower and sesame seeds.

Hot Raw Beetroot
Cauliflower with Ginger and Sesame Seeds

HOT RAW BEETROOT

Preparation time: 15 minutes Serves 4

One serving has 90 kilocalories and 4 g fat

500 g (1 lb) raw beetroot

1 tablespoon grapeseed oil

a squeeze of lemon juice

salt and coarsely ground black pepper

Peel the beetroot and put it through the julienne blade of a food processor or grate it on a coarse cheese grater or mandolin. Heat the oil in a frying pan, add the beetroot and toss it over a moderate heat for 2 minutes until the beetroot is hot but by no means cooked. Season it with salt and pepper and a squeeze of lemon juice.

Note: Raw beetroot in a mustardy vinaigrette (see page 70) is also very good.

CARROT AND POPPY SEED SALAD

Preparation time: 20 minutes Serves 4

One serving has 80 kilocalories and 7 g fat

4 large carrots

2 teaspoons poppy seeds

2 spring onions, chopped

Hazelnut Oil French Dressing (page 71)

Peel the carrots and discard the peelings. Continue to peel the carrot flesh down the length of the carrot to form thin ribbons. Set these aside. Put the poppy seeds into a heavy saucepan and put it over a moderate heat. Cover the pan and dry-roast them for two minutes. Leave the poppy seeds to cool. Mix the carrot ribbons with the spring onions and dressing. Pile them into a serving dish and sprinkle them with the poppy seeds.

APPLE, CELERY AND WALNUT SALAD

Preparation time: 10 minutes Serves 4

One serving has 140 kilocalories and 12 g fat

2 red dessert apples

French Dressing (page 70)

a head of celery, chopped

50 g (2 oz) walnuts, chopped roughly

salt and freshly ground black pepper

To garnish:

2 teaspoons roughly chopped fresh chives

This salad is the perfect accompaniment to many main courses as it is very refreshing and has an excellent texture.

Wash the apples but do not peel them. Quarter, core and slice them neatly. Arrange them in overlapping slices around the edge of a circular plate. Immediately dribble half of the French Dressing over them, to prevent them from browning.

Mix together the celery and walnuts. Add the remaining dressing, season well and pile the mixture in the centre of the apples. Sprinkle the chopped chives over the walnuts and celery.

PASTA AND RED PEPPER SALAD

Preparation time: 20 minutes — Serves 4

One serving has 300 kilocalories and 7 g fat

250 g (8 oz) pasta (preferably spirals)

2 red peppers

French Dressing (page 70)

chopped fresh sage

Red peppers completely change when they are grilled until black and then peeled: they taste better than ever. For a really special salad make this with Balsamic Vinegar Dressing (page 71).

Cook the pasta in plenty of boiling salted water to which a tablespoon of oil has been added. When it is tender, drain it well and leave it to cool. Cut the peppers into quarters and remove the stalk, inner membrane and seeds. Heat the grill to its highest temperature. Grill the peppers, skin-side uppermost, until the skin is black and blistered. With a small knife, remove all the skin. Cut the flesh into strips. Toss the pasta, pepper, dressing and sage together.

Pasta and Red Pepper Salad

Pasta with Tomato and Egg Sauce

Tabouli

TABOULI

Preparation time: 30 minutes soaking + 30 minutes drying + 10 minutes — Serves 4

One serving has 230 kilocalories and 8 g fat

- *175 g (6 oz) bulgar*
- *4 spring onions, chopped*
- *2 tablespoons extra virgin olive oil*
- *1 tablespoon chopped fresh mint*
- *2 tablespoons chopped fresh parsley*
- *2 tablespoons lemon juice*
- *½ cucumber, diced, skin and all (optional)*
- *salt and freshly ground black pepper*

There are lots of different recipes and spellings for this delicious Mediterranean salad. In France it is often made from cous-cous but in the Lebanon it is made from par-boiled cracked wheat (bulgar). The only important point is that it should be green and taste of lemon. This also makes an excellent first course.

Soak the bulgar in cold water for 30 minutes. It will expand greatly. Drain it and wrap it in a clean tea towel. Squeeze out the moisture and then spread it out to dry for a further 30 minutes. Mix the spring onions with the bulgar; use your hands and squeeze to get the onion juice to penetrate the bulgar. Add the oil, mint, parsley, lemon juice and cucumber if you are using it. Mix well, season to taste and serve.

PASTA WITH TOMATO AND EGG SAUCE

Preparation and cooking time: 40 minutes — Serves 4

One serving has 440 kilocalories and 11 g fat

- *2 large spanish onions, sliced*
- *1 tablespoon olive oil*
- *2 × 400 g (14 oz) cans of whole tomatoes, chopped*
- *300 g (10 oz) pasta butterflies or spirals*
- *1 tablespoon chopped fresh basil*
- *3 eggs, beaten lightly*
- *fresh parmesan cheese, grated*
- *salt and pepper*

Cook the onions very slowly in the olive oil. They should become soft but not coloured and this should take 15–20 minutes. Add the tomatoes, salt and pepper, stir well and bring the mixture up to the boil. Let it simmer for 10 minutes.

Meanwhile, cook the pasta in rapidly boiling water to which a teaspoon of oil and little salt has been added. When the pasta is cooked, drain it well and refresh with hot water.

Take the tomato sauce off the heat, season it, add the basil and then gradually pour in the lightly beaten eggs. The sauce should become rich and creamy. Mix a little of the sauce with the pasta, pile it into a serving dish and pour the remaining sauce over it. Serve sprinkled with a little freshly grated parmesan cheese.

KIDNEY BEAN AND SUNFLOWER SEED SALAD

Preparation time: soaking overnight + 1½ hours cooking + 5 minutes

Serves 4

One serving has 340 kilocalories and 10 g fat

375 g (12 oz) dried kidney beans or 750 g (1½ lb) canned kidney beans

2 tablespoons sunflower seeds, shelled

French Dressing (page 70)

To garnish:

chopped fresh chives

This is the perfect convenience food salad in that both the kidney beans and sunflower seeds can be kept in the store cupboard.

Soak the kidney beans overnight if you are using dried ones. Bring them to the boil in fresh water, let them boil for 5 minutes and then discard the water. Bring them back to the boil in fresh water and let them boil for at least 12 minutes; then simmer them until they are tender, about 1¼ hours.

Wash the cooked beans well and then mix them with the sunflower seeds and French Dressing. Sprinkle on the fresh chives.

MUSHROOM AND CORIANDER SEED SALAD

Preparation time: 10 minutes + 2 hours marinating   Serves 4

One serving has 90 kilocalories and 9 g fat

250 g (8 oz) button mushrooms

French Dressing (page 70)

1 onion, sliced

sunflower oil

2 teaspoons coriander seeds

plenty of freshly ground black pepper

Wipe the mushrooms, slice them fairly finely and leave them to marinate in the dressing for 2 hours.

Cook the onion until it is soft but not brown in a non-stick frying pan in the minimum amount of oil. Crush the coriander seeds with a pestle in a mortar, add them to the pan and cook for 1 minute. Cool and add to the mushrooms and season the salad well.

Mushroom and Coriander Seed Salad
Kidney Bean and Sunflower Seed Salad

SAUCES AND DRESSINGS

SALAD DRESSINGS

Preparation time: 5 minutes Serves 4

When I first became a health enthusiast I always made french dressing using yogurt in place of oil. I simply let down low-fat natural yogurt with a little water or an interestingly flavoured vinegar (not lemon juice as it is too acidic for yogurt) and added a tablespoon of suitable, roughly chopped, fresh herbs. This dressing is particularly good made with balsamic vinegar. I still rather like dressing made like this but now I sometimes use oils. Making a dressing from three parts grapeseed oil and one part good quality vinegar is fine, I think, because grapeseed oil is very high in polyunsaturated fat. If I make a dressing from a walnut or hazelnut oil I use five parts oil to one part vinegar. The quantities given below for four people still contain quite low levels of fat overall.

Another good dressing is simply to whisk a good quality oil into a fairly mild mustard; add the oil slowly and try to prevent the dressing from separating. If it does separate, put it into the refrigerator for a while and then whisk it again with a little wine vinegar. If you can't get it to re-emulsify put a little more mustard into a bowl and add the curdled dressing as if it were oil. The quantities given here are for an average salad for four people.

French Dressing:
1½ tablespoons grapeseed oil
½ tablespoon wine vinegar
One serving has 50 kilocalories and 6 g fat

Yogurt Dressing:
2 tablespoons low-fat natural yogurt
2 teaspoons water
1 teaspoon wine vinegar
One serving has 5 kilocalories and less than 1 g fat

Balsamic Vinegar Dressing:
2 tablespoons low-fat natural yogurt
2 teaspoons balsamic vinegar
a little water if necessary
One serving has 5 kilocalories and less than 1 g fat

Walnut or Hazelnut Oil Dressing:
1½ tablespoons walnut or hazelnut oil
1 teaspoon wine vinegar
One serving has 50 kilocalories and 6 g fat

YOGURT SAUCE

Preparation time: 5 minutes — Serves 4

One serving has 20 kilocalories and less than 1 g fat

150 g (5.29 oz) carton of low-fat natural yogurt
2 spring onions
1 tablespoon chopped fresh apple mint
salt and freshly ground black pepper
To garnish:
a few leaves of apple mint

This recipe calls for apple mint because it is so pretty, but any fresh mint can be used.

Mix together the yogurt, spring onions, chopped mint, salt and pepper. Pour into a sauceboat or ramekin dish and decorate with a few leaves of apple mint.

CARROT AND CARDAMOM SAUCE

Preparation and cooking time: 30 minutes | Serves 4

One serving has 18 kilocalories and less than 1 g fat

250 g (8 oz) carrots

3 cardamom pods

1 bay leaf

a little grated lemon rind

2 tablespoons 1% fat fromage frais

salt and plenty of freshly ground black pepper

This sauce can be used for all sorts of things, for example, as an accompaniment to chicken or fish dishes or as a dip for crudités. It is best made with old carrots that are full of flavour.

Peel and slice the carrots. Cook them, covered, in the minimum amount of water with the seeds of the cardamom pods and the bay leaf.

When the carrots are completely tender, drain them well, remove the bay leaf and 'whizz' the sauce in a food processor until it is smooth. Let it cool and then add the lemon rind and fromage frais. Season it to taste.

Carrot and Cardamom Sauce

Red Pepper Sauce
Tomato Vinaigrette

RED PEPPER SAUCE

Preparation time: 20 minutes + 20 minutes cooking + chilling Serves 4

One serving has 50 kilocalories and 4 g fat

1 red pepper
1 onion, chopped
1 tablespoon sunflower oil
2 tomatoes, peeled and de-seeded
1 garlic clove
a bouquet garni
6 tablespoons water
salt and pepper

This sauce is delicious and simple to make. I like it because the singed red pepper gives it the element of subversive sophistication that I am always searching for when cooking. This is excellent with fish, roast chicken and plainly cooked vegetables.

Heat the grill. Cut the pepper into quarters lengthways; remove the pith and seeds. Grill the pepper, skin-side uppermost, until it is black all over. Skin it and cut the flesh into strips.

Cook the onion in the oil until it is just beginning to soften. Add the tomatoes, red pepper, garlic and bouquet garni. Add six tablespoons of water, bring the sauce to the boil, season it, cover the pan and cook the sauce for 20 minutes.

Remove the bouquet garni and liquidise the sauce until it is smooth. Push the sauce through a sieve into a clean container and chill it.

TOMATO VINAIGRETTE

Preparation time: 5 minutes Serves 8

One serving has 105 kilocalories and 11 g fat

6 tablespoons grapeseed or sunflower oil
1 tablespoon good quality white wine vinegar
2 fresh tomatoes, chopped
salt and pepper

This is excellent with avocados, fish pâtés and cold chicken.

Liquidise all the ingredients together, push the dressing through a sieve and then liquidise it again until it is well emulsified. Season to taste.

PUDDINGS

PEARS IN RED WINE

Preparation time: 20 minutes + 1½ hours cooking | Serves 4

One serving has 70 kilocalories and 1 g fat

4 pears
300 ml (½ pint) fairly sweet red wine such as Lambrusco
300 ml (½ pint) water
1 bay leaf
4 cloves
grated rind of 1 orange
1 tablespoon ginger wine
To garnish:
toasted, flaked almonds

Peel the pears. Put them in a saucepan with the wine and water. Add the bay leaf, cloves and orange rind. Bring the liquid up to the boil and let it simmer very slowly for 1½ hours. Remove the pears and allow them to cool.

Meanwhile, reduce the cooking liquor, by rapid boiling, to half its original quantity. Let it cool slightly. Add the ginger wine. Put the pears back into the liquid. Serve scattered with toasted, flaked almonds.

REDCURRANT, MINT AND YOGURT PUDDING

Preparation time: 10 minutes | Serves 4

One serving has 70 kilocalories and 1 g fat

300 ml (½ pint) low-fat natural yogurt
500 g (1 lb) redcurrants, topped and tailed
concentrated apple juice to taste
1 tablespoon chopped fresh mint
1 egg white

This is a quick and simple, light summer pudding which is even better made with greek yogurt. It can also be made with blackcurrants.

Mix together the yogurt and redcurrants. Sweeten them to taste with a little concentrated apple juice. Add the mint. Whisk the egg white until it is stiff but not dry and fold it into the yogurt and redcurrant mixture.

Note: This should not be made more than 2 hours in advance.

RASPBERRY PLATE

Preparation time: 15 minutes — Serves 4

One serving has 55 kilocalories and less than 1 g fat

250 g (8 oz) raspberries
concentrated apple juice
4 generous tablespoons 1% fat fromage frais
a little water
4 ripe figs, cut into quarters

This is even better if you use greek yogurt instead of the 1% fat fromage frais; it comes with a higher fat content and guiltier conscience but is still relatively low in fat.

Liquidise the raspberries. Add a little concentrated apple juice to sweeten them if required. Strain the purée and pour some on to half of each of four pudding plates. Thin the fromage frais with a little water and pour it on to the other half of the plates.

Marble the fromage frais and raspberry purée together with a large fork and arrange the figs on top.

STRAWBERRIES WITH SOFT CHEESE AND BLACK PEPPER

Preparation time: 5 minutes — Serves 4

One serving has 65 kilocalories and 1 g fat

500 g (1 lb) unhulled strawberries
125 g (4 oz) skimmed milk soft cheese
a little water
freshly ground black pepper

Pile the strawberries into a serving dish. Beat the cheese and add enough water to give the consistency of a dip. Season with freshly ground black pepper.

To serve, let each diner dip strawberries into the dip and eat them with the fingers.

Raspberry Plate
Strawberries with Soft Cheese and Black Pepper

PRUNE MOUSSE

Preparation and cooking time: soaking overnight + 35 minutes + 3–4 hours chilling

Serves 4

One serving has 160 kilocalories and 1 g fat

375 g (12 oz) prunes, soaked in black Earl Grey tea overnight

pared rind of 1 lemon

1 tablespoon lemon juice

1 tablespoon concentrated apple juice

a little water

15 g (½ oz) or 1 envelope of gelatine

3 tablespoons water

2 tablespoons greek yogurt

1 egg white

To serve:

segments of fresh orange

The colour of this pudding is rather dull but the taste and texture are delicious. I thought that it would be especially nice made in a ring mould and served filled with orange segments.

Simmer the prunes in the tea with the lemon rind until they are tender. Remove the lemon rind. Strain the prunes and make up the liquid to 450 ml (¾ pint) with the lemon juice, apple juice and some water. Stone the prunes and purée them in a food processor with the strained prune juices.

In a small, heavy pan soak the gelatine in three tablespoons of water and leave it to become spongy. Pile the prune purée into a bowl. Dissolve the gelatine over a gentle heat; when it is clear and warm, add it to the prune purée. Fold in the greek yogurt. Whisk the egg white till it is stiff but not dry and fold it into the purée. Tip the mousse mixture into a wet ring mould and leave it in the refrigerator to set, 3–4 hours.

To serve, invert a plate over the mould, turn the two over together and lift off the mould. Fill the centre of the jelly with segments of fresh orange.

HOT WINTER FRUIT SALAD

Preparation time: soaking overnight + 5 minutes + 20 minutes cooking — Serves 4

One serving has 250 kilocalories and no fat

- *500 g (1 lb) mixed dried fruits, such as prunes, apricots, figs and apples*
- *1 tablespoon calvados or brandy*
- *water to cover*
- *4 tablespoons orange juice*
- *3–4 cloves*
- *1 teaspoon concentrated apple juice*
- *5 cm (2-inch) stick of cinnamon*
- *¼ teaspoon mixed spice*
- *pared rind of 1 lemon*

Soak the mixed dried fruits in the calvados or brandy and enough water just to cover them. Leave them overnight.

Pour the fruit into a saucepan, add the orange juice, cloves, concentrated apple juice, cinnamon, mixed spice and lemon rind. Bring the liquid to the boil and let it simmer slowly until the fruit is soft. This will take about 20 minutes. Remove the cloves, cinnamon and lemon rind. Serve hot; it is also nice cold.

ARRANGED FRUIT SALAD

Preparation time: 25 minutes — Serves 4

One serving has 85 kilocalories and no fat

1 large ripe mango

2 ripe passion-fruit

3 tablespoons orange juice

2 figs, cut in 8

12 green grapes, halved and pipped

8 strawberries, sliced

To decorate:

4 sprigs of mint

We often have healthy eating classes and demonstrations at Leith's School and this simple but stunning summer pudding is always hugely popular. Any fresh fruit can be used but I have suggested a combination that I find makes an attractive arrangement.

Skin and stone the mangoes. Process (do not liquidise) the passion-fruit pulp, mango flesh and orange juice together for 3 minutes. Sieve the purée on to the base of four pudding plates so that each one is well covered. Arrange the prepared fruit in a pretty pattern on each plate. Decorate each plate with a sprig of mint.

Note: If you do not have a food processor, the mango flesh and orange juice can be liquidised with the *sieved* passion-fruit pulp.

Arranged Fruit Salad

'ced Fruit Salad

Water-melon Salad

FRUIT SALADS

We often have fruit salads for pudding. They are delicious and have a negligible fat content. Recipes for something so simple aren't really necessary but here are some slightly more unusual ideas.

Green Fruit Salad: any green fruit will do, such as kiwi-fruit, green melon, green grapes and unpeeled green apples. Prepare the fruit and dress it with orange or apple juice.

Red Fruit Salad: any red fruit such as raspberries, strawberries, redcurrants and water-melon, prepared and dressed with a tablespoon of triple-distilled rose-water.

Pale Orange Fruit Salad: orange or yellow fruit such as peaches, nectarines, bananas and mangoes, prepared and dressed with the pulp of two passion-fruit mixed with 150 ml (¼ pint) water.

Orange Fruit Salad: citrus fruit such as oranges, satsumas and ugli fruit, prepared and dressed with a tablespoon of triple-distilled orange-flower water.

Soft Fruit Salad: any soft fruit such as redcurrants, bilberries and blackcurrants, prepared and dressed with a tablespoon of *crème de cassis* liqueur, two teaspoons concentrated apple juice and 150 ml (¼ pint) water.

Water-melon Salad: prepared strawberries and the flesh of a water-melon, balled or cut in small cubes, served in the water-melon shell. Dress the salad with a tablespoon of triple-distilled rose-water and decorate it with flowers such as chrysanthemum petals or gypsophilia.

Pineapple and Date Salad: fresh pineapple and dates, mixed together. Process (do not liquidise) the flesh of two ripe passion-fruit and a large, ripe mango with three tablespoons orange juice for three minutes. If you do not have a food processor, sieve the passion-fruit flesh and then liquidise the juice with the other ingredients. Sieve the purée and use it to dress the salad.

ICED FRUIT SALAD

Preparation time: a few hours chilling + 30 minutes — Serves 8

One serving has 110 kilocalories and less than 1 g fat

- *1 small melon*
- *1 papaya*
- *4 oranges*
- *125 g (4 oz) black grapes*
- *125 g (4 oz) strawberries*
- *125 g (4 oz) cherries*
- *1 red apple*
- *2 bananas*
- *lemon juice*
- *ice cubes*

This is just another version of fruit salad, but it does look very attractive. I ordered it recently at a Chinese restaurant where they sprinkled the crushed ice with a little crème de menthe.

Put all the fruit, unprepared, in the refrigerator for a few hours to chill well. Then prepare the fruit for eating with the fingers as follows.

Cut the melon into quarters, remove the skin and cut the flesh into fingers.

Cut the papaya in half, remove the seeds and skin and cut the flesh into slivers.

Peel the oranges, break them into segments and remove any pith.

Break the grapes into bunches of three or four grapes each.

Leave the strawberries whole and unhulled and wash the cherries and leave the stalks on.

Just before serving, wash, quarter and core the apple and cut it in slivers with a stainless steel knife. Peel the bananas and cut them in large pieces. Arrange the fruit on a well chilled dish and sprinkle it with lemon juice.

To make crushed ice, process the ice cubes in a food processor (check the instructions to ensure this is safe) or put them in a stout plastic bag and beat them with a rolling pin. Sprinkle the ice on the fruit and serve immediately.

APPLE JELLY

Preparation time: 10 minutes + 2–4 hours chilling | Serves 4

One serving has 140 kilocalories and no fat

900 ml (1½ pints) fresh or longlife apple juice

30 g (1¼ oz) or 3 envelopes gelatine

Buy good quality apple juice for this recipe. Any type of fruit juice in cartons can also be used, except pineapple juice which will prevent the gelatine from setting.

Put three tablespoons of apple juice in a small saucepan. Sprinkle on the gelatine and leave it for five minutes to become spongy. Dissolve the gelatine over a gentle heat without boiling it. When it is warm, mix it with the apple juice and pour it into a wet plain jelly mould or pudding basin. Chill the jelly for 2–4 hours or until it has set. Loosen the jelly round the edges with a finger. Invert a serving plate over the jelly mould. Turn the mould and plate over together, give them a sharp shake and remove the mould. If the jelly will not budge, dip the outside of the mould *very* briefly in hot water to loosen it.

Variation: Peel three oranges as you would an apple (diagram 1). Remove all the pith as you peel. Cut them into segments (diagram 2), reserving the juice. Peel and slice two kiwi-fruit and mix the slices with the orange segments. Pile the fruit and juice into the centre of the ring mould.

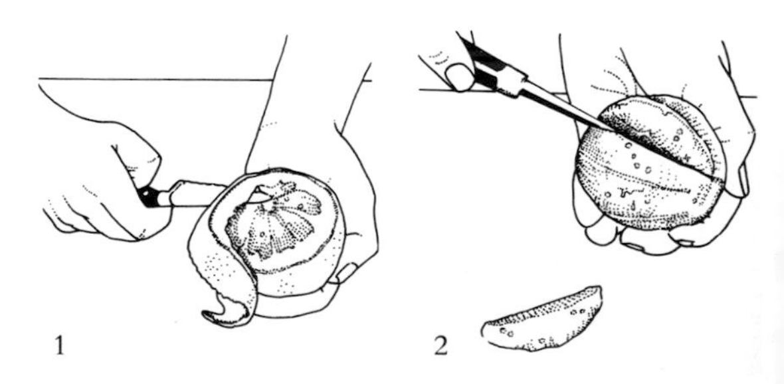

Claret Jelly
Apple Jelly
Black Coffee Jelly

BLACK COFFEE JELLY

Preparation time: 10 minutes + 1½ hours setting — Serves 4

One serving has 30 kilocalories and less than 1 g fat

600 ml (1 pint) strong black coffee

concentrated apple juice to taste

20 g (¾ oz) gelatine

To serve:

yogurt or fromage frais

I like this jelly made with no sweetening at all, but I think that most people will need the concentrated apple juice. It certainly needs to be eaten with a cream 'substitute' such as yogurt or fromage frais.

Make up the black coffee using freshly ground coffee beans and, while it is still warm, sweeten it to taste with the concentrated apple juice. Even if you like coffee without sugar, you will probably find that, as a jelly, it needs to be a little sweet. Allow the coffee to cool.

Put five tablespoons of the cool coffee into a small saucepan. Sprinkle on the gelatine and set it aside for 5 minutes to become spongy. Dissolve the gelatine over a gentle heat. When it is warm pour it into the remaining coffee and spoon it into suitable individual moulds that have been rinsed out with water.

Refrigerate until the jelly is set. This will take about 1½ hours. Turn the moulds out on to individual plates and put a good dollop of yogurt or fromage frais on each.

CLARET JELLY

Preparation and cooking time: 35 minutes + 3 hours setting   Serves 4

One serving has 75 kilocalories and no fat

- *300 ml (½ pint) claret*
- *1 small stick of cinnamon*
- *pared rind of 1 orange*
- *3 cloves*
- *1 bay leaf*
- *8 tablespoons orange juice*
- *15 g (½ oz) or 1 envelope gelatine*

Claret jelly is always a very popular pudding at Leith's School and this is similar to the one that we make but without the added sugar. I find it perfectly sweet enough but some people may like to add a little concentrated apple juice.

I had a pudding like this recently: the jelly had been poured into the base of a plate and once set it was covered with a beautiful arrangement of prepared fresh fruit.

Put the wine, cinnamon, orange rind, cloves and bay leaf into a saucepan. Place it over a low heat and leave the contents to infuse for 30 minutes. Once the pan is reasonably warm, turn off the heat and just let the wine stand.

Meanwhile, pour the orange juice into a small, heavy pan and sprinkle on the gelatine. Leave it to become spongy.

Strain the infused wine into a bowl. Melt the gelatine over a gentle heat; when it is warm and runny, add it to the wine. Stir it well and pour the mixture into a wet 600 ml (1 pint) jelly mould. Refrigerate the jelly until it sets, 2–3 hours.

To serve, dip the mould briefly in hot water for just long enough to loosen the jelly without melting it. Put a damp serving dish over the mould and invert it so that the jelly falls out on to the plate. Edge it into the centre if necessary; wetting the serving dish makes it possible to move the jelly more easily.

MANGO ICE CREAM

Preparation time: 15 minutes + 5–6 hours freezing — Serves 4

One serving has 150 kilocalories and 2 g fat

2 large ripe mangoes

a few tablespoons water

600 ml (1 pint) best quality low-fat natural yogurt

a little concentrated apple juice, if necessary

It gives me real pleasure to serve either my children or my guests this ice cream; they are really excited by it and I am cheered to find that it is perfectly possible to make a really good ice cream without using cream or sugar.

Skin and stone the mangoes. Liquidise or process the flesh, with a few tablespoons of water, until it is smooth. Push the flesh through a sieve and then beat it into the yogurt. Taste the mixture and sweeten it with concentrated apple juice if you like. Then place the mixture in the deep-freeze and leave it until it is icy and half-frozen.

Tip the ice cream into a chilled bowl and whisk or process it well. Refreeze it until it is almost solid.

Tip the ice cream into a chilled bowl yet again and break it up. Whisk or process it until smooth. Freeze it again until it is firm. Remove it from the freezer 30 minutes before serving it.

Mango Ice Cream
Peach and Banana Ice Cream
Orange Ice Cream

PEACH AND BANANA ICE CREAM WITH GRAPE SAUCE

Preparation time: 10 minutes + 5–6 hours freezing Serves 4

One serving has 260 kilocalories and 1 g fat

4 ripe peaches

2 bananas

500 g (1 lb) low-fat natural yogurt

concentrated apple juice (optional)

For the sauce:

750 ml (1¼ pints) grape juice

Ice creams made from yogurt have a more crystalline texture than conventional ones but the more times they are whisked, the smoother they become.

Peel and stone the peaches. Peel and chop the bananas. Process or liquidise together the peaches, bananas and yogurt until the mixture is very smooth. Taste it and sweeten it with the apple juice if required (it will taste less sweet once frozen). Place the ice cream in the deep-freeze until half-frozen. Tip it into a chilled bowl and whisk or process it well. Refreeze until it is half-frozen and whisk or process it again. Freeze again until firm.

Meanwhile, put the grape juice into a saucepan and reduce it by boiling to a quarter of its original quantity. Cool it and then refrigerate it. Remove the ice cream from the deep-freeze to the refrigerator 30 minutes before serving it; serve with the grape sauce separately.

ORANGE ICE CREAM

Preparation time: 30 minutes + 5–6 hours freezing Serves 4

One serving has 120 kilocalories and 1 g fat

Simply make Orange Mousse (page 94) and freeze it until firm.

Remove it from the freezer 20 minutes before serving it.

STRAWBERRY TARTLETS

Preparation time: 20 minutes + 10 minutes cooking | Serves 4

One serving has 220 kilocalories and 10 g fat

6 large sheets of fillo pastry

grapeseed oil

Pear Sorbet (page 92)

250 g (8 oz) strawberries, hulled and cut in half

Oven temperature:
Gas Mark 6/200°C/400°F

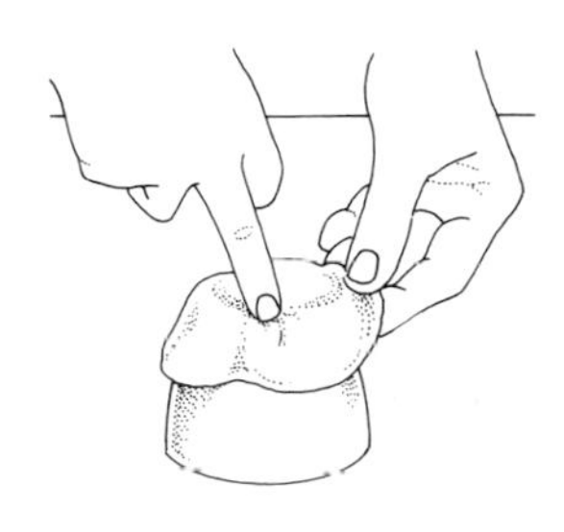

This recipe calls for fillo pastry, which can be bought fresh or frozen. When you have made the tartlets, the remaining fillo pastry can just be re-frozen. Any sorbet can be used; the combination of pear and strawberry here is unusual but perfect.

Preheat the oven. Using a large round pastry cutter, cut out forty rounds of fillo pastry. Brush the bases of eight upturned ovenproof cups with oil and cover each with a round of fillo pastry, as in the diagram. Brush the pastry with a very little extra oil and add another four rounds of pastry in the same way to each cup. Bake the tartlets for 10–15 minutes until they are a pale golden-brown. Remove them from the oven, loosen them carefully from the cups and leave them to cool on a wire rack.

Five minutes before serving, place a spoonful of pear sorbet in each fillo tartlet and arrange the strawberries on top.

PEAR SORBET

Preparation time: 15 minutes + 20 minutes cooking + 4 hours freezing

Serves 4

One serving has 60 kilocalories and no fat

2 William pears

300 ml (½ pint) water

1 tablespoon concentrated apple juice

5 cm (2-inch) stick of cinnamon

125 ml (4 fl oz) Sauternes or other sweet white wine

1 egg white

If you can find William pears they do make the best possible pear sorbet, but, failing them, Comice pears are a good substitute. Conference pears are not really suitable.

Peel, quarter and core the pears. Poach them in the water with the concentrated apple juice and cinnamon stick for 20 minutes.

Remove the cinnamon, rinse it and keep it for another use. Drain the pears and process them with the wine. Freeze the mixture until it is half-solid.

Whisk the egg white until it is just stiff. Put the half-frozen sorbet into the food processor and process it until it is soft. Gradually add the whisked egg white. It sounds surprising, but the sorbet literally doubles in bulk. Refreeze the sorbet for 4 hours. Remove it from the freezer 20 minutes before serving.

Note: If you do not have a food processor simply liquidise the wine and cooked pears and freeze them. Liquidise them again and fold in the lightly whisked egg white. Refreeze.

APPLE AND GINGER CAKE

Preparation time: 20 minutes + 25 minutes baking | Serves 4

One serving has 300 kilocalories and 11 g fat

125 g (4 oz) pear and apple spread

175 g (6 oz) plain wholemeal flour

2 eggs, beaten

3 small dessert apples, peeled and grated

50 g (2 oz) cashew nuts

½ teaspoon ground ginger

¼ teaspoon bicarbonate of soda

For the filling:

50 g (2 oz) skimmed milk soft cheese

1 tablespoon low-fat natural yogurt or 1% fat fromage frais

concentrated apple juice to taste

To finish:

a very small quantity of icing sugar

Oven temperature:
Gas Mark 5/190°C/375°F

This cake can genuinely be described as virtuous. The recipe below assumes that it is to be a tea cake. If preferred it can be the perfect accompaniment to Mango Ice Cream (page 88). If it is to be eaten as a pudding it should be baked in a 250 g (8 oz) non-stick loaf tin for 30 minutes and it does not need the filling.

Preheat the oven. Put the pear and apple spread in a large basin. Add the flour and beat it in well. Add the eggs, grated apples, cashew nuts, ginger and bicarbonate of soda and beat everything really well. Pile the mixture into two 18 cm (7-inch) non-stick sponge tins and bake the cakes for 35 minutes.

Allow the cakes to cool in the tins for 5 minutes and then turn them out on to a wire rack to cool completely. Mix the soft cheese with the yogurt or fromage frais and beat them well. Add a little concentrated apple juice to sweeten the filling. Sandwich the cakes together with the filling. Place a paper doily on top of the cake and dust the top very lightly with icing sugar. Remove the doily carefully.

ORANGE MOUSSE

Preparation time: 20 minutes + a few hours setting   Serves 4

One serving has 120 kilocalories and 1 g fat

- *300 ml (½ pint) water*
- *15 g (½ oz) or 1 envelope of gelatine*
- *190 g (6.7 oz) carton of frozen concentrated orange juice, defrosted*
- *1 tablespoon brandy*
- *300 ml (½ pint) low-fat natural yogurt*
- *2 egg whites*

Put three tablespoons of the water into a small saucepan. Sprinkle on the gelatine and leave it to become spongy. Dissolve the gelatine over a gentle heat; do not allow it to boil. When it is clear and warm add it to the orange juice with the remaining water and the brandy. Stir this into the yogurt. Refrigerate the mixture until it is just beginning to set. Whisk the egg whites until they are stiff but not dry. Fold them into the setting orange base and pour the mixture into a glass bowl. Leave it to set in the refrigerator for a few hours.

INDEX TO RECIPES

Design and layout: Ken Vail Graphic Design
Illustrations: Mandy Doyle
Photography: Laurie Evans
Stylist: Alison Williams
Food preparation for photography: Pete Smith
Typesetting: Westholme Graphics